Exploring the Galaxy

A Brief Look at Nebulae, Supernovae, and Other Wonders of the Universe

Kevin Jobson

contained within this document, including, but not limited to, errors, omissions, or inaccuracies.

Table of Contents

INTRODUCTION 1

An Ancient Interest.. 2
Seeing With Fresh Eyes 3
Constant Movement.. 5

CHAPTER 1: LOCAL HEROES 7

Sol, Our Sun.. 8
The Asteroid Belt 10
The Overachievers 13

CHAPTER 2: OTHER WORLDS THAN THIS................17

The Hunt for a New Earth 17
Earth 2.0? 20
Strange New Worlds 22

CHAPTER 3: HELLO, SUNSHINE 27

A Star Is Born 27
The Four Types of Star 30
    Giants and Supergiants 31
    Dying/Dead Stars 32
    Binary Stars 33
The Galactic Core 34
Strange Stars 36

CHAPTER 4: NEBULAE—A BEAUTIFUL MESS 39

The Different Types of Nebulae... 40
    Diffuse Nebulae 40
    Dark Nebulae 40
    Planetary and Protoplanetary Nebulae 41
    Supernova Remnants 41
The Two Hubbles 42

CHAPTER 5: GOING SUPERNOVA 47

What Is a Supernova? 47
Finding Supernovae... 50
Examples of Supernovae 53
The Next Supernova 54

CHAPTER 6: BLACK HOLES **57**

WHAT IS A BLACK HOLE? 57
WORMHOLES AND WHITE HOLES 59
SUPERMASSIVE BLACK HOLES 61
OTHER NOTABLE BLACK HOLES 62

CHAPTER 7: ONTO DARKER MATTERS **65**

WHAT IS DARK MATTER? 65
NO, REALLY, WHAT IS DARK MATTER? 67
DARK ENERGY 68

CHAPTER 8: OTHER WONDERS AND MYSTERIES **71**

COMETS 71
METEORS 74
'OUMUAMUA 76
STRANGE RADIO SIGNALS 77
ANTIMATTER 78
PECULIAR GALAXIES 79
  Hoag's Object 79
  The Radio Galaxy 80
  The Antennae Galaxies 81
ARE WE ALONE? 82

CONCLUSION **85**

REFERENCES **91**

IMAGES 91

Introduction

'Space' is a contradictory word. When we use it in our everyday lives—crawl space, parking space, shelf space—it refers to something small or only just big enough. But then, under the night sky, we look up. Now, space becomes something so massive that our brains are unable to fully comprehend the scale of it. But it is certainly the right word for what we see. There are thousands of billions of suns in hundreds of billions of galaxies, and yet if you were able to add together the mass of every physical thing in our universe, it would still only amount to about 4% of the whole. The rest of it is, quite simply, space.

It is only fitting that the word is contradictory. Space is a contradictory place. It is a vacuum, yet it is constantly expanding. The laws of physics, so iron-clad and immovable here on Earth, can be broken there. It is a place where primal forces such as gravity become so vast that they can bend light and distort time. Things exist where they should not and move in ways that, according to science, are impossible. And to begin to comprehend the size of things, we have to measure time instead of distance.

The distance between Los Angeles and London is 8,777 miles or an eight-hour flight on a plane. That is a number that we can work with and understand. However, for space, we need a whole new metric to even start to make sense of the numbers involved. For this, we use the fastest thing we know of, light. Light travels at a speed of approximately 670,616,629 miles per hour. That works out to be making the trip from LA to London 21 times *every second*. It is instantaneous as far as we are concerned. But in space, that is far from being the case.

For example, the distance from our Sun to Proxima Centauri, its closest neighbor, cannot be measured in miles, or else it would fill the rest of this book. Instead, we have to use the speed of light as a measure. Light travels about 5.88 trillion miles in a year (a trillion being 1 million million). Even at such speeds and covering so much distance, it still takes light over four years of travel from Proxima Centauri before it can be seen by us. And to be clear, this is the nearest star to our own. Other stars are much farther away.

Nevertheless, despite being surrounded by impossibly vast amounts of nothing at all, the universe is filled with wonders. Not only can we now find new objects in space more easily than ever before, but we are also beginning to understand them. And in terms of human endeavor, we are closer now than ever before to taking that first great leap out into the stars.

An Ancient Interest

We have been fascinated by the Sun and stars ever since we began to walk on this planet. Some of the earliest objects that we have found contain images to do with the night sky. There are relics that date back to the Early Bronze Age, such as ancient Babylonian tablets that detail the orbit of Venus or cave paintings that depict strange cosmic events.

Even an ancient structure such as Stonehenge in England shows our great interest in the movement of our stars. The culture at the time had no written language. Yet they still had the knowledge to make a structure of huge standing stones that would show the exact position of the Sun at certain times of the year.

The Babylonians may have been the first to have a codified science to do with the stars. Alas, not enough remains from that time to know for sure. Instead, it is the Ancient Greeks who we consider the first to 'invent' astronomy (although they certainly based most of their early findings on Babylonian concepts).

In 500 BCE, the philosopher Thales was the first to come up with a method for predicting eclipses. In 100 BCE, Hipparchus produced the first catalog of stars and named the constellations. Before long, people had identified and named all the planets and begun to chart their movements through the solar system.

As humans progressed, so did our ideas about space and the methods by which it is studied. Greek ideas remained in place until the 16th century and the Renaissance. Old ideas were challenged, and new theories arose. Until Copernicus came along, we believed that Earth was fixed in place and that the Sun orbited it. He was able to prove that we were moving.

It has taken the work of hundreds of great minds for us to reach this stage. From Plato to Isaac Newton to Carl Sagan and Stephen Hawking, we have made progress only by collaborating, sharing research, and challenging each other's ideas. The digital age that we find ourselves in now makes it easier than ever to explore space. We collect information on a massive scale to the extent that we have to share it to begin to get through it all. By using new techniques and new technology, space is closer than it ever has been. For some fortunate few, it is even close enough to touch.

Seeing With Fresh Eyes

With the dawn of the space age, our understanding of space and the universe has increased at an exponential rate. The first plane took flight in 1903. Just 66 years later, Apollo 11 was launched and put man on the Moon. The advance of computing technology has been just as swift. A modern smartphone now has more than 10,000 times the processing power of Apollo 11's guidance computer. On Earth, telescopes have gone from slender tubes that could be stored in a cupboard to vast thousand-foot-wide structures. In space, our knowledge of satellites means that we can send telescopes and recording devices out beyond our own solar system and receive signals back.

With the end of the Cold War and the dawn of the internet era, scientists of all nations are now willing and able not only to gather vast amounts of information but also to share it. The mission of NASA's Transiting Exoplanet Survey Satellite (or TESS for short), for example, is to survey nearby stars to see if they have planets (known as exoplanets) orbiting them. These planets are discovered by watching the stars and recording their brightness. If the brightness dips at any point, it is likely that there is an object between the star and the telescope, and that object is likely to be a planet. But the satellite covers and records over 85% of the sky. It is only by collaborating with each other that scientists are able to sort through the huge amounts of information available. So far, they have found almost 2,000 potential exoplanets in this way.

Other advances have been no less extraordinary. A space station (the International Space Station or ISS) orbits the planet and has been continuously occupied by humans for 20 years. We have landed robots on Mars and begun to make plans for a colony there. The Rosetta mission, which was launched in 2004, observed a comet and then landed on it in 2014 as it passed by Earth. The Hubble Space Telescope was launched into orbit in 1990 and is still there today, sending back numerous detailed and awe-inspiring images of the universe. A huge amount of information about the stars is now available, but we are in no danger of slowing our progress. The year 2020 saw the successful completion of the first privately funded space venture, sending astronauts up to the ISS and returning them safely home.

This has increased our scope significantly. We are able to look far beyond not only our own solar system but also our own galaxy and into the distant reaches of the universe. Galaxies and gamma-burst emissions have been recorded that are over 13 billion light-years away from our own. Between here and there, there are billions more galaxies. Quite how many is unclear, but we are discovering them in their thousands all the time. Or rather, we are discovering their history.

Because the evidence of what we are seeing—the light—is hundreds, thousands, millions, or billions of years old, the thing we are looking at may no longer be there at all.

Figure 1: Mars Rover

Constant Movement

Looking up at the night sky, you might be fooled into thinking that everything is calm. After all, we have known for centuries that the position of the stars can be mapped and used to navigate. But it would be a mistake to think that they are fixed in place, simply hanging in the void. The truth of the matter is that everything in the universe is moving at tremendous speeds, including us.

Spoiler warning: Fans of time-travel movies may wish to avoid the following paragraph as it ruins just about any story set in that genre. Traveling through time from one place to another would be difficult enough, but none of the brilliant albeit slightly mad scientists seem to realize that you would also need to travel through space. Earth is not in the same place as it was five minutes ago, nor is the Sun.

Earth spins at about half a mile per second and orbits the Sun at over 600 miles per hour. But the Sun is also moving, spinning as part of an arm of the Milky Way, a rotation that takes approximately 250 million years to complete. This means that the Sun is moving at about 130 miles per second. If we were to observe our solar system from a fixed point, we would watch it zoom past, the planets swirling like a corkscrew as our Sun flies through space.

The movement does not stop there. The Milky Way itself is moving, spinning like all the other galaxies, all influenced by gravity and objects with the greatest gravitational pull, such as black holes. If the theory that existence started with the Big Bang is true, the universe is still exploding. Galaxies are born and die; stars collapse and explode, and fresh ones are formed. Were you able to speed up the film, so to speak, it would be like watching fireworks, a chaos of explosions and flashes of light as the original Big Bang goes on.

So, while it may seem a still and serene place from Earth, it is worth remembering that everything is moving and subject to incredible forces. Perhaps this is why there are so many unique and amazing sights to be seen when you take a look into space.

Chapter 1:

Local Heroes

With the universe being so mind-breakingly large, it would be easy to think of our own humble solar system as somewhat small and insignificant. Nothing could be further from the truth. First of all, it contains Earth, which is as of yet the only confirmed source of life in the galaxy. That puts it at the top of the list when it comes to wonders of the universe.

Secondly, our solar system has all the best names, although this is a little unfair to the rest of the universe. Scientists realized pretty early on that there were just too many objects in space to name them all. Now, they are given numbers and designations. But by that point, we had already discovered a great many of the objects orbiting our Sun and named them. We gave them names like Hyperion, Ceres, and Calisto. The gods that inspired them are long forgotten, but their names live on in our moons, constellations, and asteroids.

Given the vast distances involved with space, the chances are that we will not be leaving our solar system for quite some time. But that is not a problem as there is plenty of solar system to go around, depending on how you measure it. Again, because the numbers get so large, we need a different unit of measurement. The distance from Earth to the Sun is 92,955,807 miles or 1 AU (which stands for astronomical unit). The farthest orbiting object in our system, a planetoid named 90377 Sedna, is estimated to orbit at 937 AU. That gives our solar system a not-too-shabby diameter of 178.6 billion miles.

Sol, Our Sun

To give it its correct designation, our Sun is a yellow dwarf star. However, the name is a bit misleading. Our Sun is far from small. In fact, it is one of the larger stars in the universe. If you compare the billions of other suns out there, the universal average size of a sun is approximately half the size of our own. Even when compared with suns of the same type, other yellow dwarf stars, our Sun measures up. It is believed that our humble Sun is in the top 10% of all stars in terms of mass. If it were hollow, it would take about 1 million Earths to fill it.

But what is all that mass made up of? Primarily, two types of gas. Hydrogen, which makes up 70%, and helium, which comprises 28%. The other 2% is made up of trace amounts of other gases and metals. The reaction at the center of the Sun, the massive, ongoing explosion that gives out heat and light, is all that hydrogen being converted into helium at a rate of 700 million tons per second. It is a process that began 4.5 billion years ago, and it will take about the same amount of time to complete. In other words, our Sun is middle-aged.

While it can feel pretty hot on Earth at times, the Sun remains a huge distance from us. The light and heat that we feel left the Sun eight minutes earlier. It produces a dizzying amount of power, almost 4 billion billion megawatts. But it is not a stable and constant reaction. There are changes and fluctuations on the surface of the Sun that are visible from Earth. These are known as sunspots, and they show up as dark patches. This is not to say that these patches are areas where the fire of the Sun has gone out. It is just that they are relatively (up to 2,000 degrees) cooler than the rest of the sun, and therefore, they show up as slightly darker.

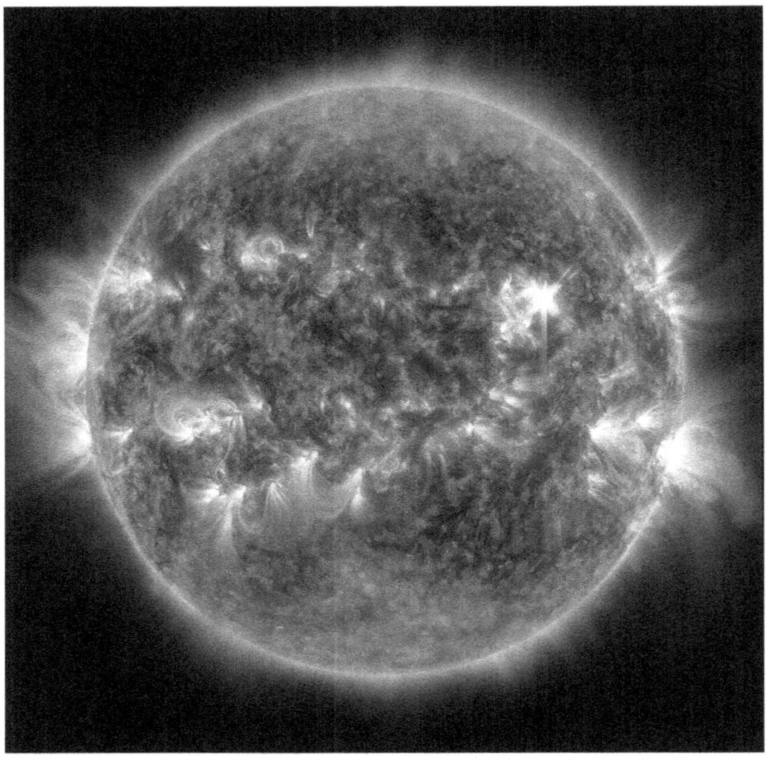

Figure 2: Solar flare

Scientists have noticed that there are established patterns of sunspot activity. Every 11 years, the amount of sunspot activity increases and then subsides. You might have thought that when there are sunspots, cooler areas on the surface of the Sun, that the Sun would have less of an effect on Earth. In fact, the opposite is true. When there are sunspots, the temperature rises. We are not yet entirely sure how or why this happens.

As well as providing heat, light, and the conditions for life on Earth, the Sun has another vitally important role. As it hurtles through space at 130 miles per second, the Sun is pumping out huge amounts of particles at high speed. This is known as solar wind, and it creates a huge bubble around the solar system, known as the heliosphere. This bubble protects our system from other particles that could, if allowed to travel through our system, have devastating effects.

The solar wind is not entirely beneficial. There is a great deal of harmful radiation that could impact us. However, Earth and the other planets in our system are protected from damage by magnetic fields. At certain times of the year, you can even see it as the Aurora Borealis or the Northern Lights. This is the solar wind battering against Earth's magnetic field.

The solar wind also makes itself visible whenever we have visitors. Comets, which are primarily made of ice, sometimes pass close enough to the Sun to partially melt. This melting causes a tail, making the comet more visible in the sky. But it is not the speed of the comet streaking through the sky that causes its tail. Instead, it is the solar wind blowing the melted fragments of dust and matter away. Think of it as if you were passing a smoking branch in front of a fan.

All good things come to an end, and in 5 billion years or so, so will the Sun. At some point, it will run out of hydrogen to burn. At this time, the reactions that take place within it will become more violent. It will swell to about 100 times its current size, consuming Earth and many of the other planets as it evolves into a red giant. Then, when all the fuel is gone, it will shrink back, far smaller than it has ever been, most likely to about the size of Earth itself. In this phase, the Sun becomes known as a white dwarf. All that remains is the core, which glows for a relatively short 10,000 years before going out.

The Asteroid Belt

One of the reasons that we are racing into space can be found in the area between the planets Mars and Jupiter. The birth of solar systems is often a messy affair. After all, they are formed by huge amounts of rock and dust that are dragged into a sun's orbit. Eventually, many of these coalesce into planets and moons, and everything calms down. But what happens to the leftovers? They become, in the case of our system, an asteroid belt.

The main asteroid belt, as it is known, is made up of millions of rocks. There is a huge variance in their size. Some could be picked up and carried by a person; others are the size of small planets. The biggest by far, making up a third of the mass of the entire belt, is named Ceres. One-quarter the size of the Moon, it was the first asteroid to be discovered. It has been orbited and mapped by the NASA satellite Dawn, and the next step is to gather samples from its surface.

But why all this interest in what is basically a bunch of rocks and debris? Well, there are two important reasons why the asteroid belt is vitally important. The first is that these are the same rocks that came together to form the planets. Here on Earth, we have been mining the precious resources found in this rock for centuries. Out there in the asteroid belt, there are huge amounts of resources that remain untapped.

How much? Well, without actual samples, it is hard to put a monetary value on the belt as a whole. Initial estimates suggest that there is $700 quintillion (i.e., 700 followed by 18 zeros) worth of value to be found there (Webster, n.d.). This translates to $100 billion for every person on the planet.

Of particular interest is an asteroid named 16 Psyche. Like Ceres, it is one of the bigger objects in the belt, and it is made almost entirely of metal. Scientists believe that it was once the core of an early attempt at a planet that didn't make it. Like Earth's core, it consists mostly of iron and nickel. But there may be even more valuable metals and, in some cases, ice. Water vapor was found on a survey of Ceres, leading scientists to believe that there was water beneath the surface (according to data that has just been released, there is, and it is salt water).

The second reason for the interest in the asteroid belt is far more ambitious. The problem with space travel is that it is both difficult and expensive to leave Earth's atmosphere. You need a staggering amount of fuel to get into space, and this leaves less room for materials or fuel for further exploration. The cost is also great, with items leaving Earth at the current cost of $3,500 per pound.

However, a space elevator could change all that. It is exactly as it sounds, an elevator that extends from the ground level into space. However, to create such a thing, there needs to be a destination outside Earth's atmosphere to arrive at. This is where an asteroid comes in. An asteroid of appropriate size could be moved, most likely towed and maneuvered by robots, and (very carefully) placed into geostationary orbit around the planet. Then, all that remains is to build an elevator that is 22,000 miles high.

It may seem like science fiction. However, not only is it possible, but people are working even now to bring it to life. The benefits for space exploration would be huge. We would no longer need rockets to move things into space. The cost of transporting supplies and building materials would drop to under $50. A base could be constructed on the asteroid, and from there, a factory. We could build ships and satellites of a whole new design, one that does not require launch and re-entry into the atmosphere. It would open up the solar system for the purposes of colonization.

Of course, we are not quite there yet. However, if we continue to advance at the rate we are currently, perhaps only a few generations from now, we will see humanity taking a huge step forward. And all of it would be thanks to the asteroid belt.

The main asteroid belt, as its title suggests, is not the only belt in our solar system. There is another, known as the Kuiper Belt. This occupies the space just past Neptune, right on the edge of the solar system, and because it is so far away, it is still mostly undiscovered. Like the main belt, it is shaped like a flattened donut and contains rocks and materials from the formation of the planets. But it is much wider, with scattered objects right out at the edge of the heliosphere.

Because there is so much of it and it is all so far away from the calming influence of the Sun's gravity, it is a bit more volatile. Rocks collide with each other and go spinning off in other directions. Sometimes, a large object will be pushed out of position and begin charting a new path. These become comets, navigating a path through the solar system's various gravitational pulls like a stick caught in the current of a river.

The Overachievers

There are countless amazing sights in our own solar system. Take Jupiter, for example, which is two and a half times the mass of any other planet. Like Saturn, it is a gas giant, and, like Saturn, it has rings, although these are much less visible. There is also a storm the size of Earth that has been constantly raging for hundreds of years, called the "Great Red Spot." Jupiter has 79 moons, some of which are no less fascinating.

Io, for example, is both the driest and most geologically active object in the solar system. There are no less than 400 active volcanoes on Io, which is about the same size as our Moon. Lava and sulfur combine to paint the moon's surface in a wide array of colors, including yellows, greens, and reds.

The moon Europa, on the other hand, has such a smooth surface that scientists believe that it is covered in ice. There may be an ocean beneath that ice, and there is also the possibility that signs of life might one day be found. Ganymede, the largest of Jupiter's moons, may also contain water. Due to its size, there would be more water than on Earth.

The reason we know all of this and continue to learn more is due to the satellites that we have released into space. Wonders in their own right, they are a testament to human ingenuity and curiosity. Without them, we would have significantly less information about the universe. And many of them have exceeded even the highest expectations.

In 1977, NASA launched the Voyager Program. Two satellites, Voyager 1 and Voyager 2, were sent out to study the planets farthest from the Sun. Voyager 1 was to concentrate on Jupiter and Saturn, while Voyager 2 was to look at Neptune and Uranus. By 1989, they had both completed their missions, providing a huge amount of data that is still being analyzed today. But that was not the end of the story.

Because they were not designed to return to Earth, the satellites continued traveling through space and transmitting data. Their mission parameters were extended three times. Eventually, in 2012, Voyager 1 passed through the heliosphere and became the first man-made object to leave the solar system and enter interstellar space. In 2018, Voyager 2 did the same.

Amazingly, both are still transmitting. They have approximately five years left before they run out of power, reliant as they are on solar energy, which is no longer effective. But their mission has run 30 years longer than anyone dreamed, and they have given us a wealth of new and vital information.

Another huge success has been the Hubble Space Telescope (or HST). Launched in 1990, it was not the first nor the only space telescope in a low orbit around Earth. However, the images that it has produced have not only had tremendous scientific value, but they have also changed the way we look at space.

Before the HST, images from space were usually black and white and blurry. Even the footage from the Moon, amazing though it was, was distorted and fuzzy. But then came Hubble, and the universe was brought to life. The photos that Hubble takes are not color images. However, the image is not the only information available. We can also measure the frequency of the light, and therefore, we can ascertain the colors that should be visible.

This changed everything. The universe began to take on new and interesting shapes. What had been a black canvas speckled with dots of white became a riot of bright shades. Great clouds of reds and yellows came into view. We gave them names based on their shapes—the

Horsehead Nebula, the Pillars of Creation, the Cigar Galaxy. This fired up the imaginations of both professionals and casual observers alike, sparking a new interest in the study of space.

Figure 3: Earth as seen from the ISS

As a consequence, the Hubble telescope has been kept going long past its expected expiration date. So far, there have been five expensive missions to service it and keep it going. It has lasted for 30 years, and it is hoped that it will last 30 more. Meanwhile, a successor is being lined up. The James Webb Space Telescope is NASA's official replacement, and it is hoped that this will be launched in 2021.

There are numerous other incredibly clever devices that have expanded our knowledge. No less than six rover vehicles have landed on Mars. The most recent of these, Curiosity, landed on Mars in 2012. It was intended to spend the next two years exploring and sampling the Gale Crater. But when in 2017, it was discovered that the Curiosity Rover was in no danger of slowing down, its mission was extended indefinitely. It is still working today.

The list goes on, and it's not merely due to the work of one space agency. The Chang'e Project is currently being worked on by the Chinese Lunar Exploration Program. The project began by putting two lunar modules into orbit around the Moon. Next came the landing of lunar rovers. The third stage will involve the construction of a research station on the Moon's south pole, and it will culminate in a crewed mission at some point in the 2030s.

It would also be a mistake to discount the work done by Russian cosmonauts during the Cold War. In 1970, the USSR's Venera Project became the first to land an object on another planet (in this case, Venus), and in 1975, it became the first to photograph images from another planet's surface. And we cannot forget the Mir Space Station, the precursor to the ISS, which remained crewed and in orbit from 1986 until 2001. Now that private companies have entered the game, we are sure to enter a new golden age of exploration.

There is surely enough within our own solar system to satiate even the most curious of minds. But, as is almost the case on Earth, eventually, we will learn all that we can. When that day comes, likely many hundreds of years from now, our attention will certainly turn outward. We will be compelled to take flight, to leave the protective bubble of the heliosphere, and to follow in the footsteps of Voyager. Out into interstellar space we will go, where there are even greater wonders to discover.

Chapter 2:

Other Worlds Than This

One of the main goals of space exploration is the search for other planets that might be capable of supporting life. This is not just a hunt for extraterrestrials. If we are going to spread through the universe and colonize the stars, it will be a great deal easier if we can find Earth-like planets to settle on. But there are planets of all shapes and sizes, including some where conditions are strange.

The Hunt for a New Earth

With untold billions of planets out there, you might have thought that finding a planet similar to our own would be akin to searching for a needle in a haystack. It's far harder than that. The haystack goes on forever, and you are only permitted to search for the needle by looking through telescopes from a distance of several light-years away.

But we can make it easier on ourselves if we bear in mind certain conditions that are necessary for life to exist. The most important thing is that the planet must have water. Water has been essential for the development of carbon-based life forms on Earth. It would be just as vital to support alien life as it would be for any visiting humans. This small factor cuts down a huge amount of time and effort when searching for planets. For water to exist, the planet needs to be at the right temperature, and that means that it needs to be within a specific distance from the sun.

The "habitable zone" for a system similar to our own is easy to figure out. If the system has a yellow dwarf star like ours, then the planet would need to be in orbit at roughly the same distance as Earth is. It can be a little hotter or colder but not by much. We know only too well the huge difference a small shift in temperature can make. The zone can shift depending on the type of sun. For small white dwarf suns, the habitable zone is much closer as the sun is putting out significantly less heat. For larger, hotter suns, the zone is farther out.

The age of the sun is something else to take into consideration. A planet might be in the habitable zone of any given system. But if the sun is still young, it will be producing much more heat. The temperature on the planet will be too high to support life. You might have thought that the opposite would apply to old, dying suns and the temperature would be too low to support life. However, this is not necessarily the case. As long as the planet is in the right zone, there is a chance that life could exist.

Figure 4: Earth as seen from the Moon

The word 'life,' of course, covers multitudes. We have a huge variety of different types of lifeforms on Earth. Everything from single-cell organisms all the way up to Lady Gaga. But life did not evolve quickly. The earliest proven evidence of life on Earth is 3.5 billion years old. Studies suggest that it may even have started a billion years before that. (This is a remarkable feat considering our own Sun is 4.6 billion years old. It means that life got started quickly.) So, if we are hoping to find aliens that walk, talk, and have an interest in science, we need to factor in the time it took *us* to get to that stage.

There are other things to take into account. Does the planet have an atmosphere to shield it from radiation? Is there a moon? We have a moon, and it is possible that this had a huge impact on the development of life. There are several other factors to be considered that, again, narrow down the possibilities.

Finding planets is tricky in itself. As previously mentioned, the Transit Method—whereby observers watch for shadows passing in front of distant suns—is probably the easiest and most successful method for detecting planets. We have discovered several thousand potentially habitable exoplanets in this way. Other methods are more complicated and require the study of the most powerful force in the universe: gravity.

Gravity, as we will see in later chapters, is the absolute ruler of space. It is stronger than any physical thing, more powerful than light, and even bends the rules of time to its will. As we learn more about it, it is also becoming a useful way of finding things in space, including planets. For while the biggest thing in a solar system, its sun, is the body that exerts the strongest gravitational pull, it is also affected by the gravity of the planets orbiting it.

This effect is almost fractional, yet it can be detected. There is a slight deviance in the movement of a sun (including our own) when a planet passes by. By analyzing these tiny wobbles, scientists are able to deduce the size and number of planets that may be in orbit.

A more complex method still is to analyze the light coming from a star. This is similar to the Transit Method but potentially more accurate. After all, some suns are huge and some planets are tiny, so we might not see a small moon against the background of a massive sun. However, we can see the effect that gravity has on that light. Like a prism passing in front of the sun, a planet's gravity and its atmosphere (if it has one) can cause tiny changes to the light.

We first began to find exoplanets in the 1990s. So far, we have confirmed that over 4,000 exist, and that number is climbing rapidly. There are many more 'candidate' exoplanets that have been found. These are readings that suggest potential finds and that need a bit more scientific power behind them before they can be fully confirmed.

Since 1990, we have made many remarkable discoveries, finding planets the likes of which we could not imagine. And the good news is that there are several Earth-like planets on that list.

Earth 2.0?

The first planet that might be able to support human life was discovered in 2007. Gliese 581c can be found in the Libra Constellation, 20 light-years away from Earth. There is a huge amount that we do not know about it. It has never been seen, for example. We do not know what it is comprised of. However, the little that we can learn is of huge value when deciding whether a planet is habitable.

Its sun, Gliese 581, is a white dwarf at the end stages of its life. It is, therefore, much smaller and less bright than our Sun. This means that the Gliese 581c is much closer to the star. It speeds around in just 27 days, making a solar year on Gliese 581c shorter than an Earth month. Some believe it is too close to the sun, right at the limit of what we consider the habitable zone.

Another issue is that the planet is likely tidally locked. This means that one-half of the planet is always facing the sun; the other half is in perpetual darkness. As a result, the surface temperatures vary wildly. One side could be a blazing desert, while the other is covered in ice.

How does this make Gliese 581c potentially Earth-like? As with the habitable zone of the sun, there may be a habitable zone on the planet. Think of it as a sweet spot between the two hemispheres where the temperature is stable and where both light and shade are options. This may be a narrow strip of land all the way around the planet, but fortunately, narrow is a relative term.

Gliese 581c is over five and a half times larger than Earth. So, even a relatively small habitable area would cover a great deal of real estate. Certainly, the possibility exists that it could support life on the fringes of the planet. However, without knowing more, it is impossible to say. Ideally, Gliese 581c would be a rocky planet. However, it could just as easily be composed of something else, such as solid iron.

The most viable candidate found so far is Kepler 438b. Found almost 500 light-years away in the Lyra Constellation, it ticks off just about everything on the checklist. It is in the habitable zone of its star, which is estimated to be only a couple of million years younger than our own Sun. Moreover, the planet is approximately the same size and mass as Earth.

The only slight downside is that Kepler 438b's sun, a red dwarf star, is a bit more violent than our own. Every 100 days, according to scientists, the planet is bathed with enough radiation that even if there were oceans and rivers of liquid water on the surface, nothing would be able to survive. However, we have not yet confirmed whether the planet is made of rock or not, so there is still a long way to go.

Such endeavors certainly make you realize how extraordinarily lucky we are to exist at all. But just because conditions are not perfect elsewhere does not mean that life cannot exist. It may simply be that it has taken a different form. The vast majority of life on Earth is carbon-based. But life could exist with other elements providing the basis. There is evidence here on this planet of sulfur-based organisms. Who is to say what our neighbors may be made of?

Strange New Worlds

Finding planets that are *not* like Earth is significantly easier. There are dozens of different types of planets. Some we are familiar with, and there are several examples within our own solar system. Earth falls into the category of terrestrial planets, as do Venus and Mars. The defining feature of these is that they have a primarily rocky surface.

Gas giants can also be found in our solar system with the giants Jupiter and Saturn. These are made primarily of helium and hydrogen, so there is no surface to speak of. As with Jupiter, you would find raging storms of poisonous gas that only became more violent the lower you descended. Eventually, gravity and pressure would force these gases into a liquid state. At some point, there would be a core of some kind. However, it is not yet known for certain what this core is made of. It may be a huge chunk of metal, much like those found in the asteroid belt.

The third kind of planet is an ice giant. Neptune and Uranus are examples of this, huge worlds covered in a thick layer of ice. This is mostly due to the fact that they are so far away. A year on Neptune, for example, would be the same as 165 Earth years.

At this point, it is worth sparing a thought for Pluto. Once considered a planet in its own right, poor Pluto was downgraded in 2006 to the standard of dwarf planet. In fairness, it is smaller than our own Moon, and there are several other dwarf planets of approximately the same size as Pluto that never previously got a mention. Eris, Makemake, and the curiously egg-shaped Haumea are all dwarf planets that exist within our solar system.

Outside of our solar system, there is even more variety among planets. It is one thing to look for traces of water on other planets. It is quite another to find one that seems to be composed *only* of water. That is the case with Gliese 1214 b. At 48 light-years away, Gliese 1214 b is several times larger than our planet, giving it the classification of a super-Earth. However, despite its size, it has significantly less mass than planets of a similar size. This leads scientists to believe that instead of being covered in rock, it is covered entirely by a single ocean. For this reason, it has been nicknamed the 'waterworld.'

It is another example of the continuing evolution of planets. At one stage, Gliese 1214 b would have been in a similar state to Europa, one of Saturn's moons. Eventually, when the Sun begins to expand, the ice on Europa will melt, and it too will become a waterworld.

The age of a planet can produce some surprising results. Depending on how close it is to its sun and what it is made of, it can take between 1 and 10 million years for a planet to form. Gliese 504 b, for example, is still in its infancy. Not long ago, cosmically speaking, it was a volatile ball of molten rock. Now, things have calmed down, but it is still cooling down. For this reason, the entire planet glows a bright pink color.

A planet's lifespan is entirely dependent on the lifespan of the star it orbits. When that star begins to change, then everything in the solar system must change with it. Usually, this means being swallowed up and destroyed. This is the fate that awaits Wasp 12b, found almost 1,500 light-years away.

Wasp 12b is so close to the sun that gravitational forces have begun to warp its shape. Instead of the traditional globe that we have come to associate with planets, it is now egg-shaped. The planet's own gravity is clinging on, but in 10 million years, the sun will eventually win the battle.

Kepler 70b has already lost this battle. Its star is currently transitioning from a red giant into a white dwarf, and Kepler 70b has been caught up in the collateral damage. It is in the process of burning up, an entire planet of flame and lava where temperatures match those on the surface of our Sun. This makes Kepler 70b the hottest planet ever found.

The title of the coldest planet goes to the unfortunately named OGLE-2005-BLG-390Lb. At just 50 degrees above absolute zero, there is no atmosphere. Any gas would immediately freeze solid. Once again, this is not the planet's fault. It is not that far from its sun, sitting in the same approximate region as Venus does in our own solar system. However, the star has long since dwindled and died, and the resulting white dwarf is unable to produce much in the way of heat or light. The name is a bit of a mouthful, which is probably why some scientists have nicknamed it 'Hoth' based on the ice planet from *The Empire Strikes Back* (Kurtz & Kershner, 1980).

It is little wonder that *Star Wars* has an influence when it comes to space exploration. After all, it had such a huge impact on popular culture and no doubt inspired in many an interest in science. That's why scientists sometimes get excited whenever they discover a circumbinary planet. These are planets that orbit not one but two suns, just like the planet Tatooine in the original film.

Some planets are made of stranger stuff. HAT P-1 is a difficult planet to pin down in terms of estimating its size. Current estimates suggest that it might be about half the size of Jupiter, which is still pretty big. It is classified as a 'puffy' planet, a gas giant with a low density. HAT P-1's density is so low that you could pick it up. If there was a lake big enough to hold it, the entire planet would float on water.

Planets that find themselves closer to the sun can be subjected to some extreme conditions. Incredibly high temperatures and gravitational pressure can lead to some strange features. Some of the most precious minerals can be found on Earth both beneath and within the rocky crust of the planet. But what if the entire planet was composed of those minerals? 55 Cancri e is one such candidate, 41 light-years away. It is believed to be a carbon planet. With pressure and time, carbon changes, which is why scientists think that about one-third of the entire planet is made of diamond.

Other valuable resources simply fall out of the sky. It rains diamonds in the gas clouds of Jupiter, for example. Lightning strikes from the constant storms that roil all over the planet occasionally mingle with carbon in the atmosphere. The result is inch-sized diamonds that fall and, eventually, once the pressure becomes great enough, turn to liquid.

You get diamonds where there is carbon to make them. But HAT P7b is a gas giant that is surrounded by what is believed to be clouds of corundum, the second hardest mineral we know of. This causes not diamonds to rain from the sky but rubies and sapphires.

HD 189733b may seem calm and blue in appearance, but do not be fooled. Sitting 45 light-years away, it orbits close enough to its sun for temperatures to reach almost 2,000 degrees F. It should be glowing red, but the blue color comes from a constant rain of glass. Sand, picked up by ferocious 4,000-mile-an-hour winds, is melted into glass. Anyone attempting to land here would probably be shredded before being boiled.

There are some planets that remain a mystery. TrES-2b is one of them. A gas giant the size of Jupiter, it can be found in the Draco Constellation some 750 light-years away. The odd thing about TrES-2b is that it is incredibly dark. There is a faint red glow emanating from deep inside the planet, but that is all. It reflects less than 1% of the light that its sun shines upon it. This makes it darker than any other planet, moon, or material known to exist.

We have, by any standard, only managed to explore a handful of the planets in the universe. Some only exist in a theoretical sense. Yet we are learning more all the time. More powerful telescopes will one day be able to photograph these planets. We have already sent messages to some; eventually, we will be able to land rovers on their surface and take a look, for the first time, at the surface of a truly alien world.

Chapter 3:

Hello, Sunshine

Suns are one of the most vital components of the universe. Without the heat and light from our own, there would not be life on this planet. We think of our Sun as a constant, something that will always be there. But while our Sun is certainly long-lived, it does have a life cycle. Like everything else, there is a birth, life, and death. But because this is a star that we are talking about, each stage tends to be a bit more dramatic than most.

A Star Is Born

For such massive and powerful objects, suns have humble beginnings. They are formed from vast clouds of dust and gas known as nebulae. These clouds hang in space, the dust within them spread throughout the nebula. They slowly accumulate more and more dust until eventually, there is a change. The more there is of something, the more gravity it has. Eventually, the cloud of dust becomes thick enough to produce its own gravitational field, and this begins a process that, once begun, cannot be stopped.

The dust clumps together and begins to attract other areas of dust around it. You might imagine that the larger clump would stay in place and dust would move toward it. But in a vacuum, gravity is a two-way street. The smaller particles exert a smaller gravitational pull. Not much, but it's enough to fractionally tug at the larger clump. This causes the center to begin spinning.

Over time, more matter is attracted to the center, which flattens out and becomes a disc. The matter that lands in this disc often causes a reaction. A flash of static electricity, perhaps, or a spark of contact. This energy is transferred into the disc, and before long, the disc is beginning to create energy on its own. The core begins to heat up and produce light. It has now become what scientists refer to as a 'protostar.'

The star begins to exert more and more of a gravitational influence on the matter around it. The vast majority of anything in the area—in our case, 99% of our entire solar system—is drawn in and goes toward feeding the growing sun. But some larger objects are only drawn part of the way toward the sun. On the way, they accumulate matter by themselves, and some achieve enough mass to avoid being consumed and, instead, achieve a stable orbit. These become planets.

By now, the core of the young sun has become a thermonuclear fusion reactor. At temperatures in excess of 27 million degrees F, it is hot enough to fuse atoms to create larger atoms. In our Sun's case, it is converting hydrogen into helium. The energy released by this process is what gives the Sun both its heat and its light. This energy blasts out of the core in the form of protons and into the second of six zones of a star, the radiative zone.

You would have thought that it would be a short trip from the core of a sun to the space outside. In fact, the opposite is true. It is a slow process. Let's not forget that a sun contains 99% of all mass in a system. The bulk of this mass is in the radiative layer, tightly packed around the core. Because of the temperatures involved, none of this is solid. It is superheated and a superdense plasma. Photons travel through this plasma via radiation. However, it is not an easy journey, and the individual photons bounce around for a long time. Scientists believe that it takes about 170,000 years to reach the next zone.

At this point, the energy meets the sun's gravitational field, and there is a change. The temperature drops significantly, meaning that the energy can no longer travel via radiation. Instead, it causes the plasma to act in the same way as a pot of boiling water. Bubbles begin to form in this, the convection zone, and float upward toward the next section. This takes place quickly, especially when compared to the thousands of years spent bouncing around the previous zone.

The photosphere is the first layer of our Sun that we can see and study. By now, the temperature has dropped from 27 million degrees to a paltry 10,000 degrees (which is still hot enough to melt a diamond). The photosphere is a gaseous layer about 300 miles thick that covers the Sun. Radiation passes through the photosphere, and in the case of our Sun, eight minutes later, we see it as sunlight.

Now comes one of science's most enduring mysteries. The Sun has its own form of atmosphere, made of plasma, known as the corona. It is the corona that produces solar flares, vast eruptions of flaming plasma that seem to coil out from the Sun like a tentacle. For reasons that no one can yet explain, the temperature increases dramatically in the corona. It climbs back up to about 3.5 million degrees F.

This is contrary to everything physics has taught us. The further from the source of heat a thing travels, the cooler it gets. The Sun seems to obey this law as far as the photosphere. But then it heats again in the corona, getting hotter when the corona gets further still from the source. This takes place in the form of solar flares, great eruptions of plasma that could engulf a planet the size of Earth many times over. The flares that seem to reach out like fiery tentacles have a higher temperature still.

If we can crack the secret of why and how this happens, it could be a huge leap forward in our understanding of how energy works. But for now, it is good to know that our good old familiar Sun still has a trick or two up its sleeve.

The Four Types of Star

Stars change a great deal over the course of their extremely long lives. Each stage is distinct from the next, and we are able to tell just by looking at which stage is which. In most cases, the star falls into one of four categories. We also measure how bright they are because this varies a great deal too. Again, most stars fall into a specific category. But do not forget, this is space, so there are always exceptions!

Young or Main Sequence Stars

These are stars that are in their prime. Starting as protostars, they have gathered enough mass and energy to begin the thermonuclear fusion reactor at their core. The vast majority of stars in the universe are in this state. The brighter they shine, the hotter they burn. But in terms of luminosity, they only place sixth out of a possible eight. They are also comparatively small compared to some of their older cousins. For this reason, most main sequence stars are known as dwarf stars.

Our Sun is a main sequence star, a yellow dwarf. The largest dwarf stars can be thousands of times larger and brighter than that. But the most common type of dwarf star—in fact, the most common type of star period—is known as a red dwarf.

As their red appearance suggests, these stars are much cooler than other stars. Their initial beginnings were the same, but they never fully went through with the fusion process. This is usually due to a lack of materials or fuel. Instead, the energy created when the star was born remains within the convection zone, simmering until it eventually runs out. However, this process takes a long time to complete. Red dwarf stars have an average lifespan of 100 billion years.

Because they produce such little light, it is often hard to detect red dwarf stars out there in space. However, our closest neighbor, Proxima Centauri, is a red dwarf and is only 4.5 light-years away.

Giants and Supergiants

Running out of fuel is a natural part of a sun's life cycle. At some point, all the hydrogen is converted and now helium becomes its power source. As a consequence, the star undergoes a rapid expansion, growing in both size and brightness. But it does not grow hotter. Instead, it cools down, and its color changes. It has turned into a red giant.

Bigger stars change in different ways. Because these bigger stars start with more mass, the reaction is different when they undergo the transition to a giant. Here, the temperature rises with the switch to helium. The star begins to output even more massive amounts of energy and burns hotter. It is so hot that it looks blue in appearance.

The star Rigel is found 860 light-years away. Yet it is so large (it holds over 15 times the mass of the Sun) and so bright (with a staggering 40,000 times more luminosity than the Sun) that it is easily one of the brightest observable stars in the night sky. However, there is another system that makes even that output look small by comparison.

Eta Carinae is a system that is found over 8,000 light-years from Earth. There was no such thing as a human when Eta Carinae began to change. But now that the light has crossed that impossibly huge distance, we have been in the privileged position to be able to watch ancient history unfold before our eyes.

In 1821, a British astronomer named William John Burchill noticed that Eta Carinae was becoming noticeably brighter. He dubbed this discovery "The Great Eruption," and to varying degrees, we have watched the star grow brighter ever since. In terms of suns, Eta Carinae is an absolute monster. Not only does it have 100 times the mass of our Sun, but it also outputs 4 million times the energy.

To quote the science fiction classic movie *Blade Runner*, "The light that burns twice as bright burns half as long" (Deeley & Scott, 1982). This is the case for Eta Carinae. Blue giants have a significantly shorter lifespan than other stars, measured in millions rather than billions of years. Scientists estimate that this star only has another few hundred thousand years to live. But given the time and distance between what happens on Eta Carinae and what we see here, it is entirely possible that the sun has already moved on to the next devastating stage of its life, the supernova.

That is the fate of most supergiant stars like Rigel and Eta Carinae. Because they are so huge, they often vaporize completely, or there is the potential for them to turn into a black hole. In this, they are the rock 'n roll stars of the universe. They live fast and die young, happier to burn out than to fade away.

Dying/Dead Stars

Once a main sequence star has transformed into a giant, the final stage is to shrink back down again. With the energy core depleted and no more fuel in sight, the size and temperature of the sun begin to diminish. The remnants of the reaction that made it a sun tend to be a superdense core of carbon. This still contains many of those protons that have been bouncing around the inside, so there is still a huge amount of energy to expend.

The exposed core of the sun is still hot, and it glows white. These white dwarfs dim over time, the light and energy within fading. In the end, all that is left is the core, a dead black dwarf. However, this is only theoretical so far. It is believed that it would take longer than the universe has existed for a star to fully run out of juice. Therefore, we do not believe that there are any black dwarfs yet.

One of the oldest white dwarf stars is named J0207. It has been a white dwarf for approximately 3 billion years. It is also a bit of a mystery because it has rings. While this is not a unique phenomenon (since we have found other white dwarfs with rings), it is a puzzle.

Any material in the solar system would presumably have been eaten up when the star entered its giant phases. Anything that did survive would eventually have been reabsorbed by the white dwarf in the first few million years. How a white dwarf has a dust ring at the ripe old age of 3 billion is unclear. It is just another question that we hope one day to be able to answer.

Binary Stars

Binary stars get their own category because, well, there's two of them. These are two or more stars that orbit each other. Usually, one is larger than the other, but both are affected by gravity. While it may sound rare, most of the stars in the universe are influenced by another. This is a huge help to scientists who can analyze the orbits of these stars and more easily calculate their mass.

Distance is no object to binary stars. Just as long as their gravitational fields have met in some way, there is a chance that they might begin to attract each other. Omicron Ceti is a system several hundred light-years away that contains a white dwarf and a red giant. These stars are about 700 times farther apart than Earth is from the Sun, but they orbit each other. A full circuit takes them about 500 years.

Others are much closer together with orbits happening at what feels like alarming speeds. Some take hours or even minutes to complete an orbit. And of course, accidents happen. In the case of Omicron Ceti, it is possible that the red dwarf will one day consume the white one. Or it might become a white dwarf itself, and that resulting loss of mass and power might have a knock-on effect on their respective orbits. Occasionally, there is a head-on collision that results in a massive explosion.

The Galactic Core

Galaxies such as our own Milky Way are shaped like spinning discs. Through the lights of the stars, you can see the spiral arms that it forms as it goes. The Milky Way, when observed from Earth, is a cross-section of one of these arms. But the center of the galaxy is bright. Could it be, as early astronomers theorized, that there is one giant star in the middle?

The answer, sadly, is no. It is, in fact, the opposite of a star. It's a supermassive black hole (which will be discussed in more detail later). This draws in and consumes anything that gets close, including suns. Within approximately three light-years of the galactic core, there are estimated to be about 10 million suns.

It is incredibly difficult to discern what is going on within the galactic core. Because the supermassive black hole is consuming everything, there is a vast amount of energy and radiation being expelled. Clouds of gas and dust surround the center, obscuring our view. More advanced radiography technology has allowed us to get a clearer view of the chaos by using X-rays. But we are still only just beginning to be able to understand what is happening in the middle of a galaxy.

Figure 5: The Milky Way

Strange Stars

KIC 8462852 (known to its friends as "Tabby's Star") briefly became something of a viral sensation in 2015. Scientists were using the transition method to search for planets, and they were studying the face of a sun to see if anything passed in front of it. They found that the light had dimmed, which was exactly what they were looking for. However, it had dimmed significantly more than they were expecting, by as much as 20%. Theories began to abound as to what was causing this. One of the more outlandish but attention-grabbing theories was that it was a huge alien structure.

A sun would make an excellent battery. All you would need to do would be to build something around it that harnesses its power. This theoretical megastructure is known as a Dyson Sphere, and it is what some people believed that they were looking at on Tabby's Star. Sadly, this is more than likely not the case. Instead, huge clouds of dust may be obscuring the view. After all, it is 1,500 light-years away. It would be understandable if something got in the way from time to time.

Another curious star is HE 0437-5439. It is not possible to tell you exactly where this star can be found. Just about every other star in the galaxy remains in a stable orbit. However, HE 0437-5439 is not sitting still. It is blasting a path away from our galaxy at over a million miles an hour.

Where this happened is harder to pin down than how. At some point, this star came into contact with something far bigger and stronger than itself, likely the supermassive black hole at the galactic center. However, this encounter was not enough to draw the star in. Instead, with gravity acting like a slingshot, it catapulted it out into the universe. No doubt one day it will come into the influence of something else, and its trajectory will likely change again. However, it is likely going too fast to achieve a stable orbit ever again. It is, quite literally, a shooting star.

The oldest star we have ever found is something of a surprise as well. When scientists first discovered HD 140283, it appeared to be over 16 billion years old. This was something of a problem seeing as how the universe itself had been dated as being only 14 billion years old. They rechecked their workings and changed the estimate of its age to about 13.5 billion years. So, while it is not older than the universe itself, HD 140283 is certainly one of the oldest stars that we have ever discovered.

Chapter 4:

Nebulae—a Beautiful Mess

"All are from the dust, and to dust all return" (King James Bible, 1769/2017, Ecclesiastes 3:21). This is a phrase commonly heard in the unfortunate event that someone dies. The author was right, but perhaps they did not know at the time quite how right they were. For not only is it the case for humans, but it is also the case for stars, planets, moons, and almost everything else. They all begin and end as dust, forming great clouds that we refer to as nebulae.

These clouds of dust and ionized gas are often huge, many light-years across. However, there is not a great deal there. An area of nebula the size of Earth, for example, might only contain enough physical matter to fill a bowl. Despite their apparent lack of substance, nebula clouds are still subject to the all-powerful gravity of the universe, and eventually, fragments of dust begin to attract each other and clump together.

Before long, a chain reaction has started. It may take millions, even billions of years to complete, but eventually, enough matter will gather and become dense enough to form a star. Billions of years later, the sun goes supernova, exploding and sending all that matter that had been so painstakingly collected back out into the universe. What starts from dust returns to dust.

The Different Types of Nebulae

The first nebula was discovered around 150 AD by the Greek mathematician Ptolemy. Over the centuries, astronomers found more and more, but not all of them were nebula. Due to the limitations of their telescopes, a number of mistakes were made. In many cases, what they believed to be nebulae were, in fact, distant galaxies outside our own.

We know far more about them now, though, enough to be able to separate them into distinct categories.

Diffuse Nebulae

This is the most common type of nebula, so named because it has no boundaries (as some of the others do). It is a cosmic mess, the clouds of dust and gas scattered far and wide. For the most part, these are visible either because they emit their own light (emission nebulae) or reflect the light from nearby stars (reflection nebulae).

However, sometimes these clouds of diffuse nebulae are incredibly dense in places. They are so dense, in fact, that they can block or even absorb light, and these are, therefore, named dark nebulae.

Dark Nebulae

You might have thought that these would be hard to detect, but it is quite easy. Due to the overwhelming number of bright objects in space, it is quite rare to see patches of darkness. These may look like they are empty, but the likelihood is that a dark nebula is blocking the view.

One of the most famous dark nebulae is visible to the naked eye from Earth. Known as "The Great Rift," it lies in space between our solar system and the rest of the Milky Way. Essentially, it is obscuring what would be a spectacular view of the rest of our galaxy, including the galactic core.

Early astronomers had several prosaic explanations for this dark patch. Due to its narrow and winding shape, the Inca called it "The Great River" and named nearby constellations after animals that had approached the river's edge to drink. The ancient Greeks believed it was the work of Phaethon, son of the Sun God Helios. Essentially, Phaethon stole the keys to his dad's chariot and went on a joyride before being struck down by Zeus, the leader of the Greek gods. They believed that the Great Rift was the path that the out-of-control chariot took across the stars.

Planetary and Protoplanetary Nebulae

As smaller stars enter the final stages of their lives, they discard all the mass that they had accumulated in their youth. This gas is flung outward from the star, but it remains partially subject to its gravity. It hangs around the changing sun as it transitions from a red giant into a white dwarf.

The name is somewhat misleading. Once again, early astronomers were not completely sure what they were looking at, and they believed that they were seeing planets. In fact, there are no planets involved since most of them have already been consumed during the sun's earlier expansion. Scientists believe that our Sun will eventually spawn its own planetary nebula in about 8 billion years.

Supernova Remnants

We will discuss supernovae in more depth in the next chapter, but they are essentially what happens when a big enough sun comes to the end of its life. Because the sun has more mass than others, two things usually happen. Firstly, the core of the sun collapses in upon itself and becomes a black hole.

At the same time, there is a huge explosion. For the duration of the supernova, the sun emits approximately as much energy as an entire galaxy. Dust and gas are propelled far and wide, covering an area of approximately one light-year.

Figure 6: The Orion Nebula

The Two Hubbles

When it comes to what we know about nebulae, we owe one man a great debt. Edwin Hubble, an American astronomer, was able to prove that there were galaxies other than our own by studying nebulae. While this had long been theorized, Hubble was the man who proved that it was true. This moment fundamentally altered our understanding of the universe.

No wonder then, that when scientists first began the project to send a telescope into space, they named it after Edwin Hubble. The Hubble Space Telescope (HST) has proved just as groundbreaking as its namesake. Thanks to its findings, we have been able to more accurately estimate the age of the universe and the size of the Milky Way. An estimated $10 billion has been spent on its creation and upkeep since it was launched in 1990. Such is its value to science.

For the rest of us, the HST has been the source of some amazing images, primarily of nebulae. One of the most famous of these is a section of the Eagle Nebula known as the Pillars of Creation, taken in 1995. The Eagle Nebula itself is a diffuse nebula in the Serpens Constellation about 6,000 light-years away, and it is actively creating stars.

The Pillars themselves are one such area in the nebula, also known as a star nursery. There are several large columns of dust and gas that are five light-years long. Within these columns are dozens of stars forming.

Of course, taking a photo of the Pillars of Creation was no simple task. The image that we know and recognize is a composite of 32 different images taken by four separate cameras. The image became so famous that the HST revisited it as part of plans to celebrate 25 years since its launch. A new, high definition image was taken, as well as an infrared image.

Another star nursery is the Carina Nebula, which contains a number of smaller nebulae made famous by the HST. At 8,000 light-years from Earth, it is one of the largest and brightest diffuse nebulae in the universe. Eta Carinae, the hypergiant blue star, can be found here.

Other whimsically named nebulae are also residents in Carina, including the Horsehead, Homunculus, and Keyhole nebulae, as well as one named Mystic Mountain. Like the Pillars of Creation, Mystic Mountain is a huge, dense mass of gas and matter where stars gestate and are born. There is even one known as The Defiant Finger. This one is shaped almost like a fist, with a single digit thrusting upward.

One of the closest and biggest nebulae (though not as large as Carina) is the Orion Nebula, just 1,500 light-years away. Most of the stars have already been born in this nursery, giving scientists a valuable insight into what happens next. But there are still others forming.

Much of the gas in the Orion Nebula has been shaped by the birth of new stars. As with our own Sun, these stars emit their own stellar winds, and the gas is often blown away by this. This gives the nebula a scattered, chaotic appearance as it is torn apart by the objects it helped create.

The HST images are colorful. But are they an accurate representation? Well, not quite. With most televisions and monitors, we use three colors—red, green, and blue (RGB)—as the basis for making up all the rest. If we did this for a nebula, we would see fuzzy and indistinct dark red clouds. This is because the dominant gas in the nebula is hydrogen, and this shows as red.

However, if we tune the image not to three colors but to three types of gas, we can fine-tune it and see significantly more detail. Most images of nebulae are tuned to SHO—sulfur, hydrogen-alpha, and oxygen. Other combinations are possible, including nitrogen and helium. It is the analysis of these gases that gives the photographs their color. Helium shows up as bright blue, while oxygen is a darker blue. These two gases are usually found where a nebula has a defined center, such as a planetary nebula.

Next comes hydrogen, which is tuned to green. Sulfur, found at the edges of the nebula, shows up as yellow and red. In some cases, when taken together, a planetary nebula could have the appearance of a big, unblinking blue eye hanging in space. These nebulae have been given appropriate names: the Cat's Eye Nebula, the Retina Nebula, and, because it has the appearance of a face surrounded by a huge, furry hood, the Eskimo Nebula.

One of the strangest nebulae to be found so far is known as the Boomerang or Bowtie Nebula. It is believed that this is a relatively young nebula in the early stages of becoming a planetary nebula. When a star begins to shed its mass as it changes from a red giant to a white dwarf, it does so not in all directions at once but from either side. This gives many planetary nebulae an hourglass shape, often like two mushroom clouds.

What is interesting about the Boomerang/Bowtie Nebula is that it is officially the coldest place in the universe. At one degree above absolute zero, even the background radiation from the Big Bang (the event that created the universe 14 billion years ago) is warmer. Clouds of gas are being blasted away from the sun at speeds of 100 miles per second. As a result, all of the heat has been dissipated, and with the sun now a white dwarf, it will never heat up again.

We are still learning. One day, we hope to learn what is going on with the Waterfall Nebula. Found 1,500 light-years away, the Waterfall Nebula has a shape that you might expect—a long, flowing trail of gas like water falling from a height. It is distinct, clearly a shape that has been formed rather than a scattered cloud like so many others. We just don't yet know what the cause of it is. There are theories that solar winds from a young star nearby are pushing the gas into a current. Whatever the reason, it is a spectacular sight, a great ribbon of light hanging in space.

All of these nebulae have been photographed and made more visible than ever before by the Hubble Space Telescope. The satellite continues to do so today, providing a huge amount of information to a wide variety of people. Anyone can apply for a timeslot to use the HST, and it has proven essential to numerous projects around the world, including amateur astronomers.

Eventually, unless someone steps in and is able to give the HST a boost, it will fall back into Earth's atmosphere and be destroyed. There will be other space telescopes in orbit by then, and they may even be more advanced. But we should never forget the work done by both Edwin Hubble and the telescope named after him. Both have uncovered many secrets of the universe.

Chapter 5:

Going Supernova

You might have thought the phrase "guest star" was something that came into existence with the birth of television and movies. After all, before their invention, stars were things that were found only in space and not causing a stir on Hollywood Boulevard.

However, the first recorded use of the phrase came much, much earlier. In 185 AD, Chinese astronomers noticed a new patch of light in the sky that they noted contained numerous colors and was approximately the size of a bamboo mat. The patch of light remained for a few months before fading. They came to the conclusion that this was a visitor to their skies, a literal guest star. What they did not realize was that they were witnessing the effects of a supernova.

What Is a Supernova?

As with many things in astronomy, early observers made assumptions about what they saw that were not quite correct. The celebrated Danish astronomer Tycho Brahe observed a supernova event in the Cassiopeia Constellation in the 15th century. At the time, it was believed that the heavens (i.e., space) were fixed and never changed. There were certainly no such things as other galaxies beyond our own. Brahe realized that this assumption was incorrect and that the event, as described in his book *De Nova Stella* (*The New Star*), must have taken place a long way from Earth. While this was clearly a landmark moment in our understanding of the universe, Brahe did get one thing wrong: He had not witnessed the glorious birth of a new star. Instead, he was seeing the terrible death of an old one.

Novae, supernovae, and hypernovae are all classified according to the size of the involved star. The bigger the star, the more massive and influential the resulting nova. A regular nova usually occurs in binary systems when a white dwarf and a red giant are in orbit. The red giant is at the stage of its life where it expands rapidly. The white dwarf, on the other hand, is starving. It has shed almost all of its mass. and now, there is no more fuel left in the tank. But it is orbiting a healthy, living star, sometimes passing close enough for some of the healthy star's gases and matter to be caught up in the hungry white dwarf's gravity.

Back when it was also a red giant, the star that is currently a white dwarf had a thick, dense layer of plasma and gas between it and the core. Any new potential source of fuel would just add to its mass, and the red giant would continue to grow. But at this time, the white dwarf no longer has an outer layer. The gases it is sucking in go straight to the core. This would be like pouring gas into a car, except instead of pouring it into the gas tank, where it is stored and fed in small amounts to where it is needed, the petroleum is poured directly onto the exposed and running engine. Before long, it explodes.

The light from the explosion burns incredibly brightly, visible in space for anything from a few days to a couple of months depending on the mass of the white dwarf. Any remaining gas surrounding the white dwarf is blasted away at speeds of thousands of miles per hour.

The same conditions can bring about a supernova. The difference between the two depends on the size of the white dwarf star. The more mass a star has, the greater the amount of energy gets released when the star goes nova. These are the biggest explosions in the universe, and as already discussed, they can cause a single star to expel as much energy as an entire galaxy for a few weeks. The effects can be devastating.

Say, for example, that our Sun suddenly went nova. You might expect that Earth and all the other nearby planets would be instantly vaporized. This would not be the case, but we would certainly not survive it. Any part of the planet that was facing the Sun would be boiled away instantly. The rest of the planet would become a molten ball of lava many times hotter than the surface of the Sun at its current temperature. With the Sun having exploded and sent the vast majority of its mass blasting out into space, its gravitational pull would no longer hold us in place. Earth would become a glowing rock, spinning aimlessly into the void.

(The good news is that our Sun is not the right type of star to go nova. We will not be consumed in a fiery explosion. We will instead be consumed by the Sun itself as it turns into a red giant and eats us. But there's no need to worry unless you plan on living for the next few billion years.)

What if we were to put some distance between us and a supernova? You might hope that a supernova that took place 45 light-years away would be safer. While we would not be affected by the explosion, the resulting burst of X-rays, gamma rays, and other radiation would bathe the planet. These might destroy the ozone layer completely, raise the temperature, or even change the atmosphere entirely. Even small amounts of radiation could result in mutations in our DNA.

Figure 7: Nebula

Scientists believe that 50 light-years would be the approximate safe distance. Fortunately for us, the likeliest candidate to go nova that we have discovered so far is 150 light-years from Earth. This is far enough away for us to remain unharmed. But we would certainly be affected. Even distant novae have had an effect on Earth. By analyzing the radiation levels and types found in deep rock samples, scientists have found iron that became fractionally irradiated at a time that coincided with a recorded nova event. Explorers drilling in the Antarctic ice have found elevated levels of nitrogen in gas bubbles. These have been dated to coincide with nova sightings as far back as 1000 AD. But supernovae have given us much more than that.

With the exception of the 26 elements that we make ourselves, everything on the periodic table of elements comes from space. Helium and hydrogen were the first, believed to be released during the Big Bang. Many of the familiar elements, such as carbon and oxygen, are made by stars. The vast majority of other elements are created during a supernova. These include iron, calcium, nickel, and cobalt.

These elements exploded out at massive velocities from the exploding star and drifted through space for a while. Perhaps forming part of a nebula, the dust and gas slowly clumped together and turned into stars and planets. In the case of Earth, those elements came together to form life. It is amazing to know that the calcium in our teeth came as a result of a star going supernova.

Finding Supernovae

With so many stars in the universe and more constantly being created, novae are relatively common occurrences. There are hundreds of billions of stars in the Milky Way alone. We currently estimate that there are at least 30 novae events in our own galaxy every year. Supernovae are much rarer, with one expected to occur once every 50 years. This makes novae pretty common. When you factor in all the stars in the universe, it means that at least one of them is exploding every second.

Unfortunately, this does not mean that the night sky is lighting up with fireworks every night. Finding novae is quite difficult. It is like trying to watch a lightning strike. If you are looking in the right direction, you will definitely see it. If you are not, it has gone before you can react. However, they are certainly different and unusual enough that if someone does see one, they usually record it.

Astronomical history is littered with sightings of new, bright lights in the night sky from as far back as 1000 BC. Seven sightings of rarer supernovae were recorded before the 1800s. With our modern equipment and understanding of the nature of a star's lifespan, we have a better chance than ever of witnessing a nova. Using historical records, we can go back and find the specific place in the universe where an event took place that was recorded hundreds of years earlier. We manage to catch about 10 novae per year in the Milky Way alone. However, due to the fact that they only happen to specific types of stars that are scattered throughout the universe, seeing a supernova is much rarer. Only once has the event been recorded from start to finish, and that happened entirely by chance.

In 2016, an amateur astronomer named Victor Buso was photographing galaxy NGC 613 to test his new telescope. At 67 million light-years from Earth, NGC 613 is particularly photogenic. It is a classic spiral galaxy, studied and recorded by numerous scientists over the years. However, Victor noticed a bright spot suddenly appearing at the edge of his view. He realized that he was witnessing something that scientists had been hoping to see—a sun 20 times the size of our own going supernova. The odds of him looking in exactly the right place at exactly the right time have been calculated as being at least 1 in 10 million.

The second type of supernova also has the potential not to be a supernova at all. This is when a star's mass begins to convert to iron because it is running low on fuel. It becomes heavier and heavier, until the point that the core becomes so dense and so heavy that it collapses in on itself and creates a black hole. On occasions, the entire sun collapses with it, quietly devoured by the new singularity. At other times, this collapse causes an explosion that results in a supernova.

Quite how this happens is unclear. After all, the core has just become a black hole, a super-vacuum that nothing can escape. Yet much of the star's outer layer is blasted out into space. This often results in the formation of a nebula known as a supernova remnant.

The shockwave from the initial explosion sends matter flying into space. Here it encounters other objects, gases, and matter that get swept along with the rest. It also heats this new matter until it creates a shell-like nebula around the original star.

If the core of the now supernova star does not collapse, it is likely to become a neutron star. Behind black holes, these are the densest objects in the universe. They are not large compared to the stars they used to be. It is estimated that they are approximately 30 km in width. However, if you were to take a piece of neutron star that was approximately the same size as an AA battery, it would weigh in excess of 3 billion tons. They also have exceptionally strong magnetic fields, 100 million times stronger than our own.

Because of the number of supernovae that have happened since the birth of the universe, it is thought that there are several hundred million neutron stars in the Milky Way. But these are not the only stars that are created as a result of a supernova. Huge amounts of matter, from iron and calcium to gases such as oxygen and carbon, go shooting through the universe. When these come into contact with the dust in distant nebula, their arrival can set off the chain of events that leads to the creation of new stars. From dust to dust, and then perhaps back to being a star once more.

Examples of Supernovae

The original "guest star" mentioned at the start of this chapter was located in the Lupus Constellation over 7,000 light-years away in 1006 AD. In addition to China, its appearance was noted all over the world. This is because SN 1006 (as the event is known) was incredibly bright. So bright that even at night, it was able to cast a shadow. It was also visible during daylight hours for a short time.

This new light in the sky did not remain constant. Monks in Switzerland noted that it changed its shape and luminosity several times. It remained a feature for three months before fading. But then the light returned, this time remaining visible for 18 months before diminishing once more.

It wasn't until centuries later that scientists managed to identify the source of this supernova. In 1965, a supernova remnant that resembled a huge red jellyfish was discovered. This was pinpointed as the source of the ancient supernova. However, there was no black hole discovered at its center. Instead, scientists believe that two white dwarf stars collided. This would explain why the event was so unusually bright.

An even brighter event was recorded in 2015. However, it is unclear whether this was a supernova or something else. Certainly, supernovae have a reputation for being bright, and so it is understandable that the event known as SN 2015L was classified as such at first. There were some factors that were unusual about this event, and they have cast doubt on what caused it.

It was certainly bright enough to fit the profile of a hypernova (a particularly massive supernova). In fact, it was twice the luminosity of any previously recorded supernova. Scientists believe that if the event had taken place in the Milky Way, it would have given off enough light to turn night into day. But this was happening in the wrong place. All the previous supernovae recorded had taken place in smaller galaxies that were still producing stars. This one, however, seemed to be in the middle of a large, well-established galaxy.

The other anomaly is that scientists have found little to no helium or hydrogen in their readings. Given that these are the elements that fuel an active star, it seems strange that there could be a supernova without them. We are still trying to figure out exactly what happened. Perhaps one day it will be officially classified as a supernova.

SN 1987A can be classified as a supernova, though it took astronomers some time to confirm it. First detected in 1987, it took place in the Large Magellanic Cloud, a small galaxy neighboring the Milky Way. Because it was found relatively early after it had happened, scientists were able to study it in great detail. They made many discoveries, including witnessing rings forming around the original star.

These rings were the shockwave caused by the nova catching up with the material in orbit around the star. It is estimated that the rings will fade away by around 2030. Scientists will, of course, be watching this star carefully as this happens, as they have been doing since the supernova's first appearance.

However, the question of what was left behind proved to be a mystery for quite some time. There was no sign of a black hole. Due to radioactive interference, it was hard to locate the neutron star that should, theoretically, have existed. But as discussed, neutron stars are incredibly small, especially when you are attempting to find it from a distance of over 1,000 light-years away. It was not until 2019, over 20 years later, that it was eventually discovered.

The Next Supernova

Despite there being innumerable stars that we cannot see, there are plenty that we can. Due to what we have learned already, we are now able to estimate which stars are likely to become supernovae based on their age, size, and location. Based on the laws of probability alone, we should be able to witness a supernova that is visible in the night sky some time in the next 50 years.

Making more accurate predictions is more difficult. In 2017, it was announced that a candidate had been discovered that was almost certainly due to go nova in 2022. Two stars in a binary system in the Cygnus Constellation were expected to collide. This had been discovered by analyzing the patterns of their orbits. By extrapolating their expected speed and position, it was possible to pinpoint to within a year the time at which they would collide.

However, to the disappointment of many, it was discovered that there had been an error in the calculations. Instead of being locked in a head-on collision, it was found that the stars were in a stable orbit. They had no plans to explode just yet.

One star that is definitely on the way out is named Betelgeuse. Found in the Orion Constellation, Betelgeuse was already the 10th brightest star in the night sky. It has been visible throughout human history as a bright red dot in the sky. Australian aboriginals wove it into their stories about the world, and sailors have used it to navigate.

There was a burst of excitement within the scientific community when, in 2019, the light from Betelgeuse dimmed significantly. There was some concern that a supernova may be coming sooner than expected. But after a few months, the luminosity of the star returned to its normal level. However, it does not change the star's fate. This supergiant star, about 20 times the mass of the Sun, is slowly dying, and at some point within the next 100,000 years—a very short time in cosmic terms—it will turn into a supernova.

At 700 light-years from the sun, this will be happening relatively close. We would certainly be able to see it in the night sky. Like SN 1006, it would shine bright enough in the night sky to cast shadows and be visible during the day. This would last for three months. Otherwise, life on Earth would continue as normal but for one large exception. One of the brightest stars in the sky will have forever gone out.

Chapter 6

Black Holes

The study of space involves a great deal of thinking about things that will never be directly seen or experienced. We will never know what it is like to walk on the surface of a planet in another galaxy, for example. The journey would take many lifetimes to complete, far longer than any human might live. Nevertheless, we strive to understand as much of the universe as we can see, and we can see a great deal. With each technological progression, our comprehension expands exponentially.

Even incredibly complex changes in space can be boiled down to things that make sense to us. An explosion, a collision, something running out of fuel. These concepts at least are simple enough to understand. It is a question of getting your head around the scale of things. Huge sizes, vast distances, and time, lots and lots of time. These are also familiar concepts.

So, how do you begin to understand a thing that you know you will never see? How do you explain how it works when its workings defy all the laws of physics that you rely upon to make sense of the universe? How can you comprehend a phenomenon when you cannot observe anything experiencing it? These are the problems facing anyone with an interest in black holes.

What Is a Black Hole?

As we have seen, the end of a star's life can be dramatic and extreme. As well as creating supernovae and neutron stars, there is the chance that a black hole could be formed. It all depends on the mass of the star. Neutron stars are relatively small and incredibly dense, but even they have their limits. The gravitational forces become so huge that the star's core can no longer hold its own weight, and it collapses in on itself.

This is the first of many mind-bending concepts that black holes have introduced to the world. How can a thing cause itself to collapse in on itself? In the world we understand, things collapse all the time. Take an old wall, for example. Wind, rain, and exposure to the elements might cause the wall to erode. Eventually, parts of it become weak. It is no longer strong enough to cope with the standard and constant pressure of Earth's gravity, so it falls down. The process is completed. It has passed from one state, a wall, into another, rubble.

If the black hole's gravity behaved in the way that we understand, it would continue to draw matter and mass toward it and never stop. It would consume everything that came close, drawing in suns, moons, and planets, growing in density and size. The only thing that could affect it would be another black hole that was bigger. Then, the two would combine and continue drawing everything in toward itself.

But this does not happen. What happens instead is something for which words are insufficient. To get close to the truth, we need a new language, the language of the infinite: mathematics. After all, numbers can go on forever. You can always half or double a number. Sure, they may get very small or very large, but there are no upper or lower limits. There are some calculations, such as the ratio of a circle's circumference to its diameter (otherwise known as pi), that go on forever.

Whatever it is that happens to the density of the core, it gets caught in a mathematical loop where the calculations to understand what is happening become infinite. This is important because as well as involving the regular three dimensions of space, it has now drawn the fourth dimension, time, into the equation.

Having begun this endless gravitational collapse, the black hole has essentially transcended the universe as we know it and become an area of space-time. At its center is something we refer to as a singularity. Because the gravity is falling in on itself, it is reasonable to assume that it is collapsing into something, hence the reason why we call it a hole. The singularity is where this happens.

Witnessing a singularity is just as impossible as the singularity itself. This is because it is obstructed by something known as the event horizon. Because the gravity is so strong, approaching a black hole would be a dangerous business. You would need to be carrying enough power to be able to pull away from it. This is known as escape velocity. The closer you get, the greater the escape velocity you would need. At some point, the gravity becomes such that you would need to be moving at more than the speed of light to get away, but according to the theory of special relativity, nothing can move that fast. Not even light can escape, and it, too, is consumed.

This is the event horizon, the ultimate point of no return. But it also means that nothing can be seen past that point because light no longer works. This affects how we 'see' black holes in space. We obviously do not see the black hole itself. Instead, we must observe its gravitational effects on other objects. Any light around the black hole would be distorted as it gets sucked in by the event horizon. It, along with everything else, is crushed by the gravity into infinite density and pulled in a long string of atoms down the infinite hole.

Wormholes and White Holes

But is there an actual hole? All that stuff must be going somewhere, right? Well, not really. You do not need a hole or any other kind of destination or end when you are dealing with an infinite equation. There is also the issue that the area is now space-time. Time may no longer work in the same way. Beyond the event horizon, a single moment may be stretching out forever.

Despite being theoretically and mathematically sound, this is a somewhat frustrating and unsatisfying answer. After all, it basically means that black holes are an anomaly where all the understandable components of the universe just get stuck in a loop and cease to function. No wonder many people have theorized that there is something else going on. All that matter is going somewhere. It's just that it may end up in an entirely different galaxy or a new universe altogether.

That is the theory behind wormholes. They are infinitely small holes that form tunnels between different places. This may be within the same galaxy, or it could lead to an entirely different universe or reality. It is even believed that travel would be possible through one of these tunnels, assuming you could find something small enough to survive. But there are a number of problems with this. What if there is a black hole on the other side as well? How could something escape the inescapable?

Step forward the white hole, the exact opposite of a black hole. Instead of drawing in matter, light, and time, a white hole would spew it out. It would be a one-way exit in the same way that the black hole is a one-way entrance. Perhaps it is a phenomenon in another universe, an alternate reality where they study this strange object that seems to produce an infinite supply of matter from nowhere. Perhaps they exist within our own universe. We simply have not found them yet.

It may be that we cannot find them because they do not exist yet or because they have already happened. Time within a black hole would no longer work the way we expect. It could be that the matter that is sucked into a black hole is transported back through time and shot out of a white hole so that it might one day be sucked back into the same anomaly.

This, like everything else, is a theory. We have so little to go on, but we are learning more all the time. We have satellites pointed at specific black holes and are watching to see what falls into them. We will not be able to see the exact point at which they pass the event horizon. But we can see how the matter reacts to being dragged to its doom, and this will provide further insight.

Supermassive Black Holes

You might have thought that finding black holes would be difficult. But it is pretty easy. There is a large one at the center of each galaxy, including the Milky Way. These are known as supermassive black holes, and they contain the same amount of mass as millions of suns.

How these are formed remains the subject of much conjecture in the scientific community. Some believe that they came into existence at the moment of the Big Bang. Over time, they slowly gathered more and more mass, becoming supermassive over billions of years. Others believe that the first stars themselves were supermassive. Thus, when those stars came to the end of their lives, the black holes left behind were of similar size.

Some of these anomalies are breath-taking in size. The black hole at the center of the Milky Way is known as Sagittarius A*. To us, it is pretty large. However, we have found supermassive black holes millions of light-years away that are 2,500 times bigger. Because we cannot see the black hole, the only way to calculate its size is to measure the gravitational effect it has on things around it. Eventually, it is possible to estimate where and how large the event horizon is.

For Sagittarius A*, the event horizon covers an area of approximately 17 AU (AU, if you remember, stands for astronomical unit and is the distance from Earth to the Sun). The black hole found in the middle of the NGC 3842 galaxy, several million light-years away, is much larger. That monster's event horizon would be the same distance as Earth would travel around the Sun 200 times. The event horizon is the point of no return, but a black hole of that size would affect gravity over a distance covering light-years.

Other Notable Black Holes

While they can be large, other black holes can be relatively small. The snappily titled IGR J17091-3624 can be found 28,000 light-years away in the Scorpius Constellation. Scientists believe that this black hole may have only a third of the mass of the Sun.

Just because it is small does not mean that it is weak. In fact, IGR J17091-3624 is producing some strong forces. The disc of matter that is gathering around the black hole is spinning at incredible speeds, causing winds of up to 20 million miles per hour. This may be too fast for the black hole to consume much in the way of matter. Anything caught in its gravity would likely spin around a few times and be flung off out into space in another direction.

Despite being among the strongest forces in the universe, black holes can still be knocked around. Occasionally, galaxies collide with each other. This can cause huge problems, with established gravitational orbits suddenly being challenged by gravity from other places. Even black holes can be torn from their regular position in the galaxy and sent out into space.

These so-called "rogue black holes" are quite a scary prospect. Given that they are impossible to see in the first place, tracking them could be close to impossible. If a rogue black hole with a mass several times that of our Sun were to come past our solar system, it would likely doom us all.

Given the high number of seeming contradictions that we have encountered already, it should come as no surprise that black holes can also be one of the brightest things in the universe. Mass gathers in a disc around a supermassive black hole as you would expect. Dust and gas are drawn in and consumed, but other particles are spat out.

If you think of the disc as an equator, these particles are fired off into space from the north and south poles. They are moving at such speed, close to the speed of light, that they heat up and glow, often shining brighter than anything else in the galaxy. These are known as quasars. A quasar located 30 light-years from Earth would be brighter than the Sun.

There are rare occasions when black holes collide with each other. Before this happens, they spin around each other, getting faster as they get closer. Eventually, at close to the speed of light, they finally slam into one another. This releases a huge burst of energy, 50 times more than is contained in a galaxy. But these are black holes. There is no other matter but themselves, no rock, no gas, no light. Therefore, the only thing that this collision can produce is a gravitational wave.

This is a ripple in space-time that slightly distorts the universe and is of great interest to science. If the source of a gravitational wave can be discovered, it makes mapping the surrounding stars and systems that much easier. It also tells us more about how gravity itself works and how it affects everything else. Unfortunately, it takes events of the scale of black hole mergers and supernovae for us to notice them since we do not see them often. But as we develop new techniques to measure such things, it will not be long before gravitational waves become a regular part of our observations.

Chapter 7:

Onto Darker Matters

It seems that the more we learn about space, the more we realize that we are only just scratching the surface. The moment that we looked beyond the boundaries of our own solar system, we discovered that there were millions of other suns and systems all around. The same thing happened when we looked beyond our galaxy, and we found billions more. And now that we are studying these galaxies, attempting to make sense of their composition and movements, we find that there is still a huge amount that we do not know.

What Is Dark Matter?

Our study of gravity has advanced in leaps and bounds. Through its study, we can discern whether a sun has exoplanets in orbit around it. We can locate black holes and figure out how much mass objects in space have. Having started to catalog and categorize as much as we can find, scientists have found that there is a problem. The numbers do not add up. And given that mathematics is, as we have seen, the only real way to comprehend much of what we find, this is a large problem indeed.

This first began to be noticed over 100 years ago. Scientists were beginning to calculate both the mass and speed of galaxies. This was done by adding the combined mass of the visible stars in a galaxy and measuring their speed by watching their movement relative to other objects. The problem was immediately clear. Based on their findings and what they knew about gravity, there was no way that many galaxies had enough mass to hold themselves together. According to their calculations, they were moving far too fast and should have torn themselves apart.

Other problems began to arise. One of the ways in which we detect objects in space is by using a technique known as gravitational lensing. This occurs when light leaving a distant object, say a nice, bright quasar, encounters something with a great deal of mass on its way to being observed from Earth. As we know, gravity is stronger than light, and often, it pulls the light toward the massive object. This bends the light in the same way as a lens. The stronger the pull, the more lensing that we see.

Scientists were finding that the amount of lensing did not correspond with the mass of the objects that they could see. Before long, they were able to start mapping the areas where they would expect to find something, but to their dismay, there was nothing there to find.

More mysteries began to emerge. There were anomalies in cosmic microwave radiation. Some galaxies in clusters seemed to be missing over three-quarters of the mass they should have had. Over and over again, gravitational effects were being observed that did not fit with what could be seen.

The only explanation was that there must be a great deal of mass that they could not see. This mass came to be known as "dark matter." As we studied more and our techniques improved, two things became clear. Firstly, they were not finding the missing mass by regular means. It was not simply a case of looking in the wrong place or suddenly finding it hidden behind something else. The extra weight that was holding everything together was simply not revealing itself. The second issue was that according to their numbers, there was an awful lot of this dark stuff. Like, five times more dark matter than visible matter.

Dark matter is invisible. It neither gives off nor absorbs light, and it does not interact with the electromagnetic field that covers all other things. It emits no X-rays, radio waves, or any other kind of radiation. It is not composed of atoms. The only effect that it has on the visible universe is through gravity.

A cynic might greet this news with suspicion. After all, it would be a more convenient solution than suggesting that we had simply gotten the math wrong. But this evidence has been gathered by numerous means, all observing the galaxy for different reasons and using different methods. To explain one away as a mistake would be easy. You could even figure out an alternative hypothesis. But so far, there is no alternative solution that could cover all of these issues that is better than the concept of dark matter. As Sherlock Holmes once said, "After you eliminate the impossible, whatever remains, however improbable, must be the truth" (Conan-Doyle, 1890).

No, Really, What Is Dark Matter?

Establishing that dark matter is almost impossible to detect has not stopped scientists around the world from attempting to do just that. The current thinking is that dark matter comprises subatomic particles. These are pieces of matter that are smaller than atoms. Most particles as we understand them are known as baryonic particles. They are made of protons and electrons. However, since protons and electrons react with the universe in traditional and measurable ways, the particle that we are looking for is unlikely to be composed of them.

Instead, other hypothetical particles have been suggested. Some of them have interesting names, such as Weakly Interacting Massive Particles (WIMPs) or Gravitationally Interacting Massive Particles (GIMPs). Discounting them from the list of possibilities is as important and exciting as finding that they are made of dark matter. Anything that narrows the search is good news.

If such particles exist, then to create the sort of mass that dark matter is exerting on the universe, millions of them would need to pass through every square inch of Earth every second. This means that in theory, they can be found. To do this, particles are smashed into each other under laboratory conditions. The resulting explosions are studied in the hope that they can eliminate all other particle types until they are left with the one they are searching for: dark matter.

You need to go to great lengths to attempt to detect these particles. Or rather, great depths. On the surface, Earth is constantly bombarded by protons and other particles that have come from all corners of the universe. Readings taken at sea level would be subject to massive amounts of interference. It would be like attempting to study ripples on the water in the middle of a storm.

To take cover from this constant bombardment and to drown out as much background noise or radiation as they can, scientists go deep underground. Disused mines, huge shafts, and other installations deep under the ground in the USA, Europe, China, and India are where these experiments are carried out. Even the Large Hadron Collider, the world's most powerful particle accelerator located deep under the Swiss Alps, has been brought in to help with the search.

Thousands of hours put in by hundreds of researchers on equipment that has cost billions of dollars over dozens of years have so far found … nothing. The truth behind dark matter remains as elusive as the stuff itself. Which is a shame because dark matter is only a small part of the problem.

Dark Energy

Scientists in the 20th century came to believe that the universe was started as the result of the Big Bang and was still expanding, albeit at a slower rate. However, in 1998, a study produced a somewhat different result. Scientists were studying a distant supernova, calculating its distance from us. Since this supernova had happened billions of years ago, when the universe was still young, the distance would give us an indication of how fast the universe was expanding.

The problem for scientists was that the supernova had happened much farther away than they were expecting. According to the math of such things, if the universe had been expanding at a slower rate, the sun's supernova should have occurred much closer. But based on the actual distance and with more experimentation in other areas, it became clear that the universe's expansion was not slowing down. It was, in fact, speeding up.

Whatever was causing this acceleration was counteracting the effects of gravity—the one force that, up until now, had beaten everything else. Stranger still, whatever this was, it had not been around forever. The universe's expansion had been slowing down. But then, when the universe was about 8 billion years old, this mysterious force began to accelerate the universe's expansion. It is still accelerating now.

If we thought we did not know much about dark matter, we know even less about dark energy. It also means that the universe, if it does end, may not end the way we thought. At one point, we believed that it would end in the Big Crunch. This would be the opposite of the Big Bang, when all the mass and acceleration of the universe suddenly reverses, and everything is pulled back to the center. This would likely result in a second Big Bang and a whole new universe.

Instead of a Big Crunch, there might be a Big Rip. This would be caused by the universe expanding at such high speeds that it eventually tears itself apart. Even time itself could be torn apart. We don't know what that might look like, but it is not likely to be good.

There is another alternative to solving the issue of dark matter, and that is to simply make it go away. Given that it was barely there in the first place and that after years of searching, no sign of it has been found, this is not as difficult as you might imagine. All it takes is a small adjustment to the theory of general relativity.

This was a theory developed by Albert Einstein that observed that the gravitational relationship between two masses is created as a result of a warping of space-time. These observations were based on the movements of our own solar system. But what if the rules of gravity are not constant and, in fact, are different in other systems and galaxies? If this is the case, then there would be no need for a mysterious, invisible type of matter.

It remains to be seen whether dark matter will ever be found or if we decide on an alternative understanding of the universe at a later date. But for now, dark matter and dark energy are possibly two of the biggest mysteries that the universe has offered us so far.

Chapter 8:

Other Wonders and Mysteries

Comets

Of all the strange things that we have noticed happening in space, comets are probably the most well recorded. After all, there is nothing quite like them that appears in the night sky. Early observers, unaware that the lights they saw above them were a mix of planets and distant suns, would have seen a new star appear. It would only be there for a short time, but it was clearly distinct from other stars because it had a tail. Or, as the ancient Greeks saw it, long hair.

They passed across the heavens with enough frequency that they became a rare but noted feature of life. For centuries, they were seen as portents of doom or political unrest. They were studied by healers who believed that there was a connection between the stars and medicine. Knowing when a comet was or might be sighted was considered a more auspicious time for treatment.

These ill omens were associated with the deaths of kings and natural disasters right up until the late 17th century. Sir Isaac Newton was the first to understand comets, but it is the name Halley that we most associate with the phenomena. Edmond Halley studied the records of various historical sightings and began to plot their paths. He soon realized that some of these comets were taking similar routes across the night sky, and he theorized that they might all be the same comet. Based on his findings, he predicted that a comet would be seen in the night sky in the year 1759.

Sadly, Halley did not live to see whether he was correct. He died in 1742. But sure enough, the comet did return, and so it was given his name. Halley's Comet is probably the most famous of all comets. It appears in the 11th century Bayeux Tapestry, a historical record of the invasion of England by the Normans in 1066, and has been appearing in our skies every 75 years. Its appearance in 1986 caused a huge stir, firing up the imaginations of schoolchildren, amateur astronomers, and scientists alike. This was the first time that we had satellites and modules orbiting Earth, and we were able to gather a huge amount of information. It will next be seen in 2061, making it the only comet that, in theory, is visible twice in a single human lifetime.

Comets range in size from a couple of hundred meters to several miles wide. They are composed of dust, gas, and ice. As a comet approaches the Sun, it heats up, and the gases begin to escape. This tail makes it appear as if the comet is speeding through space or even the upper atmosphere. What is happening is that the solar wind is blowing the gas away.

These comets orbit the Sun, but not in the same way as anything else. They take a much longer path, interacting not only with the gravitational field of the Sun but also the planets that they pass. For this reason, a full circuit of the solar system could take anything from a few years to several thousand.

In 2014, our understanding of comets increased dramatically with the European Space Agency's Rosetta mission. This was a probe that was sent close to the comet known as 67P/Churyumov-Gerasimenko. Rosetta watched as the comet approached the Sun and began to heat up.

More remarkable still, the probe had a small lander named Philae. This landed on the surface of the comet. It was by no means a perfect landing. Because the surface of the comet was a mass of pitted and jagged rock, there was no smooth landing zone. The lander bounced and ended up on the side of a cliff with its solar panels obscured by overhanging rock. This meant that the lander had only two days to work before running out of power.

Those two days were not wasted because the probe and lander had a wealth of different equipment aboard. There were numerous spectrometers, thermal imagers, cameras, and microscopes that were recording information throughout the mission. Even today, scientists are pouring over the data that was gathered, making discoveries all the time. It was found, for example, that the water discovered on the comet was different from the water we have on Earth, which leads to more debate about how Earth got water in the first place.

We have discovered over 6,000 comets, with more being found all the time. This is just a fraction of the potential number that is out there. On the front edge of the heliosphere, the Sun's protective bubble, is a theoretical area known as the Oort Cloud. This is believed to be a large area of asteroids that are being pushed along in front of the heliosphere like dust before a broom. Within this cloud are a trillion asteroid-like bodies that sometimes collide with each other or are influenced by something else's gravity. They move out of position, and sometimes, they enter the Sun's orbit, becoming comets.

Comets crashing into the planet and wiping out almost all life on Earth have been the subject of books and movies for many years. After all, this would not be the first time it has happened. Approximately 66 million years ago, a comet measuring nine miles across hit what we now know as Chicxulub, Mexico. The resulting change in climate is widely believed to have wiped out 75% of all life on the planet, including most of the dinosaurs.

Comet Swift-Tuttle is the one that worries astronomers. This is a large comet that comes worryingly close to Earth. If they were to collide, the resulting explosion would be 27 times larger than the impact that wiped out the dinosaurs. For this reason, scientists consider it one of the most dangerous objects in the solar system.

Smaller, less devastating comets have crashed into Earth. Around the world, there are a hundred or more craters. Many of these are believed to have been created by comets or asteroids. What are the chances that a comet might stray toward us and cause a cataclysm? Well, taking into consideration all of the impacts we have suffered so far, it appears that it only happens once in every 30,000 years. The reality is that it could happen at any moment. It is such a concern that there are telescopes and cameras that are pointed out into space looking for them. The sooner we learn that a comet might be coming right at us, the better our chances of survival.

Meteors

You would not think to look at it, but Earth is under assault. An estimated 250 million objects weighing 15,000 tons are arriving from space at 45,000 miles an hour and hurtling themselves into our atmosphere *every single day*. Fortunately for us, the vast majority of these meteors or meteoroids burn up before ever landing. Some of them, however, do make it all the way.

Most of this material comes from the asteroid belt. Small rocks or fragments of dust are disturbed in various ways. By collisions or by the gravitational pull of a larger object, they leave a standard orbit and can spin off into space. From there, they could get caught in Earth's gravitational pull. Occasionally, pieces of material from a passing comet's tail are drawn toward Earth. These often provide visible meteor showers. The meteors glow brightly as they burn in the upper atmosphere.

Some of these meteor showers are predictable. Every July, the path of Earth's rotation brings it close to a trail of debris left by our old enemy, Swift-Tuttle. Comet Swift-Tuttle comes past Earth every 133 years, last making the trip in 1992 (it will next be seen in 2126). Because it is so large, it leaves a trail of dust and small rocks in its wake. As Earth comes close to this trail, some of it gets attracted by our gravity and begins to fall into it. This creates what is known as the Perseid Meteor Shower. In terms of cosmic events, the Perseid Shower is one of the most reliable astronomical events a person can witness. Every year, thousands of amateur astronomers are glued to their telescopes to watch the show. At the peak of the shower, up to 60 objects an hour can be visible.

Figure 8: Hyperion

Most of the Perseid meteors burn up 50 miles or more above the surface. Some larger objects make it through the atmosphere but not necessarily all the way to Earth. They make it through most of the atmosphere, but closer in, the air gets thicker, and the meteor burns brighter. In some cases, it even explodes. This is known as an "air burst."

In 1908, there was a vast explosion in Siberia near the Tunguska River. The forest nearby was devastated, with nearly 80 million trees in an 83 square mile area being completely flattened. Hundreds of miles away, windows shattered, and people were blown off their feet by the shockwave. Seismic recorders as far away as Scotland registered the event.

This explosion was believed to have been caused by a meteor that exploded in the air rather than hitting the ground. Another such event was recorded recently in the region of Chelyabinsk Oblast, Russia. This was a meteor approximately 65 feet long, which, in 2013, exploded in the air, injuring hundreds of people and causing damage to no less than six different cities. The blast was over 20 times stronger than the atomic bomb that fell on Hiroshima during World War II.

Fragments of the now exploded meteor were found. It was of a type known as chondrite, formed when small molten blobs of metal were drawn together at the accretion stage of a planet's development. It contained about 10% iron, which is considered low for a meteor of that type.

‘Oumuamua

Astronomers are still puzzling over this object that briefly visited our solar system. At over half a mile long but only a few hundred feet wide, ‘Oumuamua looked a bit like a big stone carrot. It was first spotted in 2017, speeding through the galaxy. Because it moved so fast and was such an odd shape, it was named ‘Oumuamua, Hawaiian for ‘scout.’

This scout was not from our galaxy. The last time it had encountered any stars or planets had been over a million years before. It caused an immediate stir because it seemed as if gravity was not the only thing steering this object. Despite much speculation that it was a spaceship of some kind, the conclusion was that ‘Oumuamua was instead a comet. Small jets of escaping gas were slightly altering the comet's trajectory as they melted.

The opportunity to learn more about 'Oumuamua has passed. It has already left our galaxy and continues its lonely journey out into space.

Strange Radio Signals

We 'see' the universe in numerous ways other than just with our eyes. An analysis of infrared, X-ray, radiation, and magnetic fields provides a huge amount of information from galaxies and stars that are far too distant to study with a telescope. Because of this, we are uncovering new mysteries and wonders all the time. This includes radio signals that seem to be coming from deep in outer space.

These radio waves are not the same as the ones we usually interact with. We have not suddenly tuned into Radio Alpha Centauri. These are a pulse of radio waves that last, at best, a few milliseconds and are known as fast radio bursts, or FRBs. As well as being short, they are also incredibly weak, which makes finding them difficult.

FRBs were first discovered (or perhaps noticed would be more apt) in 2007. But by going back over old data, it turned out that we had been recording them for years, as far back as 2001. The 2007 discovery, the Lorimer Burst, appears to have originated in the Small Magellanic Cloud, a small galaxy neighboring the Milky Way.

Other bursts have been discovered throughout space, including our own galaxy. However, scientists have no idea what is causing them. Whatever it is, it would need to create a huge amount of energy to propel the signal far enough to be heard on Earth, 80 times the amount that our Sun generates in a year. Many believe that something as powerful as a supernova might be responsible. However, several of the signals have come from the same location. This might mean that solar flares are responsible.

Whatever they are, we are listening for them. Hopefully, in time, we will come to learn more about their cause and origin. For now, these radio signals from space remain a mystery.

Antimatter

The center of our galaxy is a busy place. As well as billions of suns and a supermassive black hole, there is something that is producing vast amounts of antimatter.

Antimatter is similar to matter (i.e., the physical 'stuff' of the universe), with one exception. All the electrical charges are the opposite. For example, a matter atom would have a nucleus with a positive charge and would be surrounded by electrons. An antimatter atom would have a nucleus with a negative charge and would be surrounded by electrons with a positive charge—positrons. If a piece of matter comes into contact with a piece of antimatter, both vanish in a bright flash and a huge explosion. The amount of energy released would be over 100 times hotter than the Sun.

It may sound like science fiction or as strange a thing as dark matter, but we have proved antimatter exists. We even use it, creating positrons to help use medical scanners. But according to most accepted theories of the Big Bang, as much antimatter as matter should have been created when the universe was born.

As you are reading this and not currently disappearing in a bright flash, the evidence is clear that this is a mostly matter-based galaxy. This begs the question: Where's all the antimatter? If there is as much of one type of matter as there is the other, we should be seeing more contact.

It turns out that there is a huge amount of interaction between matter and antimatter. In 1997, scientists turned on a new type of gamma-ray observatory. Gamma rays are like X-rays in that they are electromagnetic radiation. Gamma rays occur when the nucleus of an atom decays, for example as the result of a matter/antimatter collision.

To their surprise, scientists found antimatter right in the heart of the Milky Way. Something was causing huge amounts of matter to be converted to energy at a rate of 500 trillion tons per day. The resulting plume of gamma rays blasts out from the top of the galactic core of the Milky Way, covering 3,500 light-years.

Observing this antimatter collision is one thing. Explaining what is causing it is quite another. We have no idea what is responsible for this constant stream of antimatter appearing at the heart of our matter-based galaxy. There have been various theories. Black holes, supernovae, ancient neutron stars, and even dark matter have been posited as the source. As of yet, we still have no idea what is causing it.

Peculiar Galaxies

Hoag's Object

Hoag's Object is a galaxy located some 600 million light-years away. When it was first spotted by astronomer Arthur Hoag in 1950, he was not quite sure what he was looking at. A large yellow sun surrounded by a ring of light. At first, he thought it might be a small planetary nebula. Then he considered the idea that the star he was looking at was a quasar and that the ring of light was gravitational distortion. It was not until 2002, when the Hubble Space Telescope took a look, that the third of his guesses was confirmed. Hoag's Object is a galaxy.

Like almost all other galaxies, Hoag's Object has a bright center at its core. But unlike almost all the others, it has no rings. Instead, there is a narrow ring of young stars around the edge. Between that edge and the core, there is almost nothing else there.

There have been many theories as to how this ring galaxy came to be formed, but so far, nothing completely fits. One popular idea is that another galaxy came blasting through Hoag's Object, and the middle part of the galaxy got swept away. Another possibility is that something collided with the core and caused an explosion of mass that pushed everything out to the edges. However, neither of these ideas work. If another galaxy had come crashing in, we would see further evidence of the collision. The core is the wrong shape to have been involved in a crash. All others that have been found have a more ellipsoid shape.

There is one further strange thing about Hoag's Object. While the center area is almost empty, there is one object to be found within. Another galaxy, tiny by comparison, but this too seems to have an empty center. One unique galaxy is strange enough, but a strange galaxy with another strange galaxy within it? This one will have scientists scratching their heads for many years to come.

The Radio Galaxy

Centaurus A is less of a mystery. In fact, it seems to be doing everything possible to tell us all it can. As galaxies go, Centaurus A is one of the loudest. It is bright, the fifth brightest galaxy that we have found so far. Under the right conditions, and if you happen to be in the southern hemisphere, you can even see it from Earth with the naked eye.

As well as light, Centaurus A is also emitting vast amounts of other radiation, including radio waves. These are not to be confused with the incredibly short, fast radio bursts discussed earlier. It is just that there is far more radio radiation than visible radiation coming from this galaxy, and so it is named Radio Galaxy.

At some point, about 500 million years ago, a large galaxy consumed a smaller one. The supermassive black hole at the center of the larger galaxy is still feeding. In other words, there is still a ring of hot gas that is falling into the black hole's event horizon. Particles are blasted out of the top and bottom of the black hole at ridiculous speeds and spread out like great wings. These wings are over 100 light-years across.

Other evidence of the collision can be found in this curious galaxy. There are remnants of supernovae caused when the two galaxies collided, and there is also a nebula in which there is a population explosion of new stars. This phenomenon is known as a starburst.

The Antennae Galaxies

One collision currently in progress is happening in the Virgo Supercluster about 45 million light-years away. Two galaxies have met, and they are now in the process of forming a new, larger galaxy. Right now, things are a bit of a mess. There is a huge tail of suns and nebulae resembling the antenna on an ant's head that gives the galaxies their name.

Some of this tail will eventually catch up with the center. The rest has been freed from the gravitational pull of the core and is now on a new path through the universe. A few hundred million years from now, the Antennae Galaxies will look like a regular spiral galaxy.

There are no less than five supernovae found in the Antennae Galaxies, not to mention areas of starburst. But also of interest are the areas rich in minerals such as xenon and silicon. It is believed that for life to flourish on other planets, these minerals need to be present. Some areas have significantly more of these vital minerals than we have in our own solar system. Perhaps, in a few hundred million years when things have calmed down a little, life will flourish somewhere.

Figure 9: The Antennae Galaxies

Are We Alone?

With all those galaxies, with all their suns, planets, and moons, surely there must be life out there somewhere. Intelligent life and perhaps even civilizations more advanced than our own. So, how is it that we have not found any yet?

Believe it or not, we have not been looking for long. While the idea of traveling to other worlds and meeting people there has been a concept in fiction for most of human history, it was not until the 20th century that we embraced the idea that these other worlds might be other planets. Authors such as H.G. Wells, Jules Verne, and Edgar Rice Burrows were the first to delve into the realm of science fiction. Since then, it has captured our imaginations like nothing else.

Imagining alien life is one thing; finding it is quite another. To search space for aliens, you need equipment, and scientists and astronomers are busy using theirs to unlock the secrets of the galaxy. While the idea of finding life on other planets would likely be the biggest breakthrough in human history, people are reluctant to fund the search for "little green men."

However, a small and dedicated group was not put off. They formed SETI, the Search for Extraterrestrial Intelligence, and began looking into space. Often, this was during time borrowed from other projects using their equipment. But over time, more money has been invested in the search, and SETI's scope has been expanded.

The best way to detect life on other planets is by scanning radio waves. After all, a careful scan of our own radio waves from deep space would almost certainly confirm the existence of Taylor Swift, let alone intelligent life. However, despite all of our efforts, we have found nothing so far, though it seems we may have come close at least once.

In 1977, an astronomer at Ohio State University was monitoring recordings of radio waves. A 72-second long narrowband (i.e., a radio signal with a bandwidth of less than 10 kHz) signal was received from the Sagittarius Constellation. Amazed by what he heard, the astronomer circled the printout which displayed this information, and he was so excited that he wrote 'Wow!' in the corner. This became known as "the Wow Signal."

Unfortunately, the signal was never found again despite numerous attempts to look for it over the next 40 years. There was no information contained in the transmission, and while there are numerous theories as to what caused it, no answers have been found. Nevertheless, this is our closest proven brush with what might be an alien civilization.

If we do not find them, it is possible that aliens might find us. We are certainly not hiding ourselves away. We have sent messages to several potentially habitable galaxies for all manner of reasons. The Voyager probes, for example, launched in 1977, both contain a golden record. This is a copper record disc (what we today know as vinyl), together with the means to play it and instructions for its use etched into the surface.

On the record are numerous things that our fellow space explorers would find useful. Mathematical equations, star charts, and photographs of our solar system have all been included. But it also has photographs and sounds from Earth, music from (among others) Chuck Berry and Bach, and even an hour of recorded human brainwaves.

Our hope is that anyone we encounter is as curious and open about the universe as we are. Only by working together could we hope to overcome the huge barriers between us. The Voyager probes have already left our solar system. Perhaps, one day, many centuries from now, they will enter another. For now, however, it seems that space is ours alone to explore and try to comprehend.

Conclusion

The future for space exploration is bright. We are looking outward in more ways and from more angles than ever before. Every day, we find something new. In the days it took to write this book, a probe found saltwater deposits on the planetoid Ceres, two schoolgirls from India discovered a completely new asteroid, and a private company put two men into space and brought them back with reusable rockets.

These are just the headline stories. In the background, researchers are making discoveries not only of objects out in space but also of new ways to look at such objects. Our advances in robotics and computing have made us eager to learn what can be achieved. There is a renewed interest in the Moon, with no less than three separate projects to put new landers there.

Mars is also a subject of great interest. New countries are getting involved in space exploration. In addition to NASA and the European Space Agency, both India and the United Arab Emirates are planning missions to Mars. Before long, the biggest problem facing scientists will be gridlock caused by the number of rovers on the planet.

We are looking at the asteroid belt, selecting targets of interest, and hoping to take samples. 16 Psyche, the strange metal asteroid in the belt, will be probed. Scientists are hoping to understand its nature, whether it was once a planetary core. Further out, we plan to send probes to Jupiter and to its moons Europa, Ganymede, and Calisto. But all of this is just the beginning of our ambition.

Now that we live in an age where some corporations have greater wealth and power than most nations, it should come as no surprise to learn that they also have an interest in space. In some cases, their interest is our interest. There are companies that are investigating, planning, and even testing the possibility of commercial space travel.

Space tourists are not a new thing. In the first decade of the 21st century, several private individuals made the trip off the planet to the ISS, courtesy of the Russian Space Agency. No one knows exactly what these space tourists paid for their 10-day trip, but it is believed to be over $20 million per ticket.

The aim is to make this a more affordable luxury, though even with the most generous estimates in terms of cost, it would still be a luxury. Tickets, which can be bought in advance, range anywhere from $60,000 to $250,000. As of yet, no successful commercial flight has left the atmosphere. But some of the vehicles that they intend to use have made successful flights, so it cannot be long now.

Figure 10: Apollo 11 Moon Landing

If we are this close to the stage where anyone, not just highly trained scientists, can go into space, it is not hard to imagine the future. Bigger space stations, more people living off the planet. Eventually, colonies on the Moon and perhaps Mars. Before long, people may live most of their lives either off the planet or in space. Eventually, someone will be in the unique position to be born somewhere other than Earth.

As we spread out into our solar system, our bodies will eventually undergo changes. A person who is born and grows up in a zero-gravity environment, for example, would look different from people born on Earth. Our bodies are currently molded by our gravity. A person who had only ever known weightlessness would have a different bone density and musculature. Bringing them down onto a planet could even kill them, so it is possible that some of us would learn to live only in space.

Living on other planets with different gravities would present similar challenges. Mars has just 38% of the gravity that Earth does. A person born on Earth would have problems, their bones and muscles weakening. They would develop heart problems. A person born on Mars might not be able to cope with Earth's gravity. Over a long enough period, a new species of human might evolve.

In the longer term, it is only a matter of time before we are able to identify another planet that we could potentially live on. Getting there would entail a journey many lifetimes long. For this, we would need seed ships and colony vessels either capable of holding its occupants in stasis for the duration of the journey or big enough so that many generations of humans can live there. At this stage, we may have developed a mastery over our own genetic code. We can alter ourselves either to make the journey through space more manageable or to prepare our bodies for the conditions we might face on arrival. At this stage, we would no longer be *Homo sapiens*. We will have become *Homo galactus*.

We will, however, have to be careful. Humans have the terrible habit of leaving a mess everywhere they go, and space is no exception. In this case, we can be partially forgiven. In our rush and excitement to get into space, we did not consider the fact that some things would, by necessity, be left behind. But it is already causing us problems.

There are currently over 2,000 active satellites in orbit around the planet. Sadly, there are also 3,000 defunct ones. These are obsolete or broken satellites that have nowhere to go. They continue orbiting Earth. These are a hazard because a collision with one could be disastrous, even fatal if there are humans aboard a vessel.

But a satellite would be a relatively big target. There are smaller problems. Each rocket that leaves the atmosphere, for example, loses components along the way. Many of these larger sections re-enter the atmosphere and either crash down or burn up. But many smaller pieces stay floating in space. Even tiny fragments, like a piece of metal or a fleck of paint, could be disastrous.

The odds of hitting one of these pieces of space junk are pretty high. Several times, the International Space Station has had to move out of the path of incoming space junk. Given the cost of fuel, this is an expensive exercise.

We have even left a mess on the Moon. Around 50 unmanned probes, three moon buggies, and almost 200,000 kilos of other material have been left behind. There are also some more whimsical items, such as a piece of art by Andy Warhol and three golf balls. With luck, one day all of these items will be retrieved and put on display in the Lunar History Museum. For now, they're just a mess lying around.

Steps are already being taken to find a solution to the mess we have left. During the Cold War, the US and USSR tested missiles by firing them at satellites in space. Sadly, the resulting explosions only resulted in more space debris. Shooting them out of the sky is not an option. Other solutions have a more naval feel to them. Harpooning or netting rogue satellites from orbit could be an option.

It remains to be seen whether we learn to respect our own planet before seeking out others or whether our reckless actions will force us into the stars. For now, and for most of us, our feet remain planted on the solid rock of Earth's crust. We can only look up and dream. But as we have seen from our own recent past, those dreams can become reality, given time. In the meantime, there is so much still to discover and learn. We still have much to learn about what we have already found. Each breakthrough opens doors to new opportunities. Who knows what wonders of the universe wait out there to be discovered?

References

Conan-Doyle, A. (1890) *The Sign of Four* [Novel]. Penguin Classics.

Deeley, M. (Producer) & Scott, R. (Director) (1983). *Blade Runner* [Motion Picture]. United States, Warner Bros.

King James Bible. (2017). King James Bible Online. https://www.kingjamesbibleonline.org (original work published 1769).

Kurtz, G. (Producer) & Kershner, I. (Director) (1980). *The Empire Strikes Back* [Motion Picture]. United States, 20th Century Fox.

Moon to Mars. (2011). NASA. https://www.nasa.gov/topics/moon-to-mars

NASA Earth News. (2016). NASA. https://www.nasa.gov/topics/earth/index.html

Solar System and Beyond. (2019). NASA. https://www.nasa.gov/topics/solarsystem/index.html

Technology. (2019). NASA. https://www.nasa.gov/topics/technology/index.html

Webster, I. (Creator), Asterank.com.

Images

Figure 1: WikiImages. *Mars Rover* [Image]. https://pixabay.com/

Figure 2: Skeeze. *Solar Flare* [Image]. https://pixabay.com/

Figure 3: WikiImages. *Earth as seen from the ISS* [Image]. https://pixabay.com/

Figure 4: WikiImages. *Earth as seen from the Moon* [Image]. https://pixabay.com/

Figure 5: Adam Derewecki. *The Milky Way* [Image]. https://pixabay.com/

Figure 6: WikiImages. *The Orion Nebula* [Image]. https://pixabay.com/

Figure 7: WikiImages. *Nebula* [Image]. https://pixabay.com/

Figure 8: WikiImages. *Hyperion* [Image]. https://pixabay.com/

Figure 9: WikiImages. *The Antennae Galaxies* [Image]. https://pixabay.com/

Figure 10: WikiImages. *Apollo 11 Moon Landing* [Image]. https://pixabay.com/

www.ingramcontent.com/pod-product-compliance
Lightning Source LLC
Chambersburg PA
CBHW071455030726
47593CB00003B/1014